B. Knopf

LUDWIG WITTGENSTEIN
An Introduction to His Philosophy

LUDWIG WITTGENSTEIN

An Introduction to His Philosophy

by

C. A. van Peursen
Professor at the State University of Leyden

Translated from the Dutch
by Rex Ambler

A Dutton  *Paperback*

NEW YORK
E. P. DUTTON & CO., INC.
1970

First published 1970 in the United States
by E. P. Dutton & Co., Inc.
All rights reserved. Printed in the U.S.A.

Copyright © 1965 by Dr. C. A. van Peursen
English translation with author's revision copyright © 1969
by Faber and Faber Limited, London

This book was originally published by Het Wereldvenster,
Publishers at Baarn, Holland, under the title *Ludwig Wittgenstein*

Acknowledgements for Quotations

In translating this book from the Dutch, the translator has nearly always used the established printed English translations or texts where Wittgenstein is quoted directly. The only (rare) exceptions are where Professor van Peursen has made a special point with reference to the original German text and the translator has thought it would obscure the point to give the printed translation; e.g. he has rendered the German literally as 'the mystical' in place of 'what is mystical'. Where Professor van Peursen has quoted passages from the untranslated work, *Philosophische Bemerkungen*, in his own Dutch version, the translator has worked directly from the original German.

Acknowledgement is due to Messrs. Routledge and Kegan Paul Ltd., the publishers, for permission to quote from *Tractatus Logico-Philosophicus* translated by D. F. Pears and B. F. McGuinness; and to Basil Blackwell, Publisher, for permission to quote from the following: *Notebooks 1914–1916* edited by G. H. von Wright and G. E. M. Anscombe; *The Blue and Brown Books*; *Remarks on the Foundations of Mathematics* edited by G. H. von Wright, R. Rhees and G. E. M. Anscombe, translated by G.E.M. Anscombe; and *Philosophical Investigations* edited by G. E. M. Anscombe and R. Rhees, translated by G. E. M. Anscombe.

Acknowledgments for Quotations

Contents

LUDWIG WITTGENSTEIN
An Introduction to His Philosophy

CHAPTER ONE

Thinking Aloud

WITTGENSTEIN'S LIFE AND PHILOSOPHY

'I WALK. I think. I say something. What am I actually saying with such words? Who thinks, walks, speaks? Am I right when I say that it is *I* who walk or have a pain? Who or what can "I" refer to? I have a pain in my foot. Then I can point to my foot. Can I say, I have a pain in your foot? Can I have my pain in your foot or your pain in my foot, or can I have your pain in your foot? What has gone wrong in these sentences? I could say, my pain is always here, pointing at the same time to my foot. But suppose that we were sitting here in this room in front of a large mirror. I am sitting in the middle. I feel the pain in my foot and I can just see my foot, not beneath me, but over there in the mirror. I can then say, I have a pain in my foot, *there*. Can I also say, I am thinking in my head, that there are thoughts in my head? If I now say that I have a pain in my foot over there—pointing to my foot in the mirror—and if I turn out to be mistaken—the foot I am pointing to is not mine at all, but someone else's—can I also be mistaken about thinking? How do we use language and where do these puzzles come from? . . .'

Here is the kind of 'thinking aloud' that any of us might have indulged in at some time or other. It is also a rough sample of the way in which Wittgenstein used to philosophize and of how, throughout his writings, he is able to remind the reader of his own problems of thought and language. The passage is not a literal reproduction of his thought, but some inaccurate notes jotted down from memory after one of his seminars at Cambridge in 1946. He sat in the middle of a fairly small group—a grey-haired man with sharp features and a lithe body, which gave the impression of his being tall. Yet we still saw him as the young philosopher, logician and idealist—all in one—just as he appears in one of the best-known portraits of his earlier period. Wittgenstein had the gift of taking a statement and turning it over and over in his hands to discover every shade or variation of meaning and every connection with other forms of language. He made us share in his questioning, his experiments of thought, and the tension was felt by everyone present. He would take a statement that seemed to us sometimes remote and opaque. He would then unravel the linguistic tangles in every direction, and we were given the impression of a confusion of possible and impossible ways of speaking without any fixed network of connections being apparent. And yet it was precisely such a network that Wittgenstein had from the outset been concerned to discover. In his earliest period he was trying to bring to light the hidden logic of thought and speech and he therefore constructed, by means of symbolic logic, a network that was held up as a norm or requirement for the language of philosophy. Later, however, it was no longer a logical network but rather the criss-cross lines of a map which held his attention. In one of his later works he goes so far as to say that he has no other wish than to sketch out the landscape. He wishes to find his orientation in the reality given in language, thought and action, that is, in the forms of human life, and not to force this organic whole into some fixed scheme.

Wittgenstein's speculations, his thinking aloud, appear sometimes, as in the instance I gave to begin with, to be trivial. In fact they are not, for they revolve always around quite fundamental questions of philosophy. In the example I gave he was

WITTGENSTEIN'S LIFE AND PHILOSOPHY

dealing with Descartes's *cogito ergo sum*, 'I think, therefore I am.' The questions of thought and existence form a continuous line which runs through the whole of his work. His style is extremely aphoristic: for the most part, brief, detached sentences, which may or may not be numbered, or a series of compact theses, but seldom a flowing argument. In this he reminds one strongly of Heraclitus, who similarly tried by way of aphorism to unearth the confusion of the multifarious uses of language from the far from obvious, often concealed expressiveness of the *logos*: meaning, word, speech. Thus Wittgenstein raises classical philosophical problems partly because the idealistic trend of his life, however difficult it may be to express that in language, proved nevertheless to be the driving force of his philosophizing.

Ludwig Josef Johann Wittgenstein was born in 1889 in Vienna as the child of a well-to-do family of Jewish origin. His father was an engineer, but the Wittgenstein family had strong artistic leanings. His parents and some of his brothers and sisters—Ludwig was the youngest of eight children—were very musical. Johannes Brahms often visited their home. The one-armed pianist Wittgenstein, for whom Ravel wrote his piano concerto for the left hand, was a brother of Ludwig. Ludwig himself made a number of sculptures and designed a house for his sister which is still to be seen in Vienna. Later he also gave support, from his own means, to the well-known poets Rainer Maria Rilke and Georg Trakl. Wittgenstein had not only an artistically sensitive nature, he was also particularly nervous. He walked sometimes with hasty, irregular steps and would often in discussion get unusually excited. His eccentric disposition has become well-known and has given rise to many anecdotes, some of them quite unjust, as for example that he gave his seminars lying on his back on the ground and staring up at the ceiling. A vague fear possessed him that he might become mentally ill, and in a statement quoted later (p. 113), he says that understanding is for ever surrounded by madness. All this, however, formed the background to his immense originality, and even his geniality, which were soon to be noticed by his teachers.

After finishing at the primary school he went to the secondary school at Linz, to which a boarding-school was attached. Among the subjects taught at this school was philosophy, for which a textbook was used that was written by a pupil of the Austrian philsopher Meinong. This philosopher, who was in correspondence with Husserl, Russell and Moore, investigated the relation between thought and reality from the point of view of the 'meanings' of words as used in language—a theme that Wittgenstein was also to be concerned with. In 1906 Wittgenstein finished at the secondary school and went to study engineering, initially in Berlin, later in Manchester. He was greatly interested in aeronautical problems in the technical field, especially in the construction of propellers. This involved a good deal of mathematical study and revived his interest in the foundations of mathematics. It is understandable that he should already have acquired an interest in philosophy and, in particular, made a study of Schopenhauer's work *Die Welt als Wille und Vorstellung*. At the same time he came into contact with the work of more scientifically and logically minded thinkers. Both worlds of thought, the more idealistic and metaphysical on the one hand and the more logical and positivist on the other, had an influence on the young Wittgenstein, but continued, as it were, to live separate lives. In his first main work he was to mark the one off very sharply from the other, in his later works to bring about their integration. However, there is always a positivist strain in his thought, for he never allows himself to transgress the boundaries of meaningful and analysable language.

During his period of study in England he spent many vacations on the Continent, taking the opportunity to visit leading scholars such as Gottlob Frege, who was professor of mathematics at Jena and was largely concerned with its philosophical problems. It was Frege who aroused his interest in the philosophy of mathematics and logic and advised him to study under Bertrand Russell in Cambridge. Together with A. N. Whitehead, Russell had written *Principia Mathematica*, a logical study of the foundations of mathematics, which was in many respects influenced by Frege's work. In an autobiographical work that Russell published some years ago he writes of how much the contact with this eccentric, but extremely gifted, student has meant for him. He maintains, moreover, that Wittgenstein's earlier work, with which Russell himself had had much to do, remains of considerable value, but that he is unable to follow or appreciate his later development. Another professor with whom Wittgenstein had much contact and who himself attended seminars given later by Wittgenstein was G. E. Moore, who was in touch with the Austrian philosopher Meinong, and who sought by careful analysis to clarify the meaning of philosophical terms. We need to mention, finally, that one of Wittgenstein's friends at this time was J. M. Keynes, later to become a famous economist.

Wittgenstein made several journeys during his life to Norway, where he spent much of his time in a lonely, self-made hut, living a hermit's existence, putting his thoughts on to paper. He was doing this already in 1914 and when in that year the World War broke out he left for Austria to serve in the army. In his rucksack he carried an exercise-book in which he would make philosophical jottings. He continued to use it when in 1918 he was made a prisoner-of-war by the Italians and kept for some time in Italy. Even at this time he was able to produce a paper from these jottings, which Russell persuaded him to publish. It appeared originally in the year book *Annalen der Naturphilosophie*, and was published as a book in England in 1922. Russell wrote a foreword and the German text was published alongside the English translation by G. K. Ogden assisted by F. P. Ramsey. The translation was somewhat strained, although it had been checked and approved by Wittgenstein. So at least it appeared when Wittgenstein's handcorrected proofs were brought into a discussion that had been evoked by an entirely new and better translation (by Pears and McGuinness), which appeared a few years ago. The title of the book—*Tractatus Logico-Philosophicus*—matches the title of the original year-book publication—*Logisch Philosophische Abhandlung*—but was not conceived by Wittgenstein himself; it was suggested to him by Moore, or according to some by Ogden. The allusion, of course, is to a work of Spinoza, *Tractatus Theologico-Politicus*. There is also a similarity in logical structure between Wittgenstein's *Tractatus* and Spinoza's chief work, *Ethica ordine geometrico demonstrata*.

The *Tractatus* is a particularly difficult work. Within the small compass of twenty thousand words he tackles the whole range of philosophical questions and tries, moreover, as he says in his foreword, to hit the nail on the head and to find, on all essential points, the final solution of the problems. He makes use of symbolic logic and often discusses technical problems without indicating their background in Frege's work and especially in *Principia Mathematica*. Wittgenstein's style, moreover, is extremely aphoristic and sometimes appears disjointed. Essentially, however, we would do better to compare the book, as Stenius does, with a musical composition where the *Leitmotiv* eventually becomes evident throughout the many various modulations. The work has been misunderstood in many respects. Wittgenstein himself contends that even Frege, Russell and Moore failed to understand it completely. However, the influence of the work has been the greater for that. In particular, his positivistic conception of language and thought has influenced the 'Vienna Circle', a group of philosophers and physicists who met under the leadership of the philosopher Moritz Schlick and drew up a programme for a logical language embracing all the sciences. Among the members of this group, which met in the twenties, were Rudolf Carnap, subsequently professor in the United States, Herbert Feigl, the mathematician Kurt Gödel and for a short while the young English philosopher A. J. Ayer.

The form of neopositivism which developed between the two world wars under the name of logical positivism, or logical empiricism, differs from Wittgenstein's views on two points. With regard to the first, Wittgenstein held, along with Russell, that the logical and positive language of the exact sciences and of philosophy mirrored reality. Thus the simplest elements of a statement mirror atomic (i.e. simple) constellations in reality. This logical atomism, to be discussed further in the following chapter, is not to be found in this form in logical positivism. A second difference is that Wittgenstein recognizes the metaphysical, i.e. whatever lies beyond sense experience, even though he denies that it can be a meaningful subject of philosophical statements. (This point is more fully dealt with in Chapter Three.) Otto Neurath, a member of the Vienna Circle, represents logical positivism when he remarks that one must indeed say nothing metaphysical, but that this is not being silent *about* something: the metaphysical is rejected entirely.

Wittgenstein never belonged to the Vienna Circle, though members of the Circle did seek him out and often their discussions were, indirectly, influenced by him. But with the last words of the *Tractatus*, Wittgenstein himself had said farewell to philosophy. He was preoccupied with questions which, according to his own view in the *Tractatus*, could not be answered or even formulated—questions of what he was to do, of how, with his idealism, he should tackle the most ordinary problems of life.

On his return from the prisoner-of-war camp he immediately gave away the wealth he had inherited from his father. He trained to become a teacher and until 1926 taught in village primary schools in Austria. The interest in language which had been evident already in the *Tractatus* and was to be decisive for the whole of his later work showed itself here as well. It was not, of course, the language of philosophy which concerned him, still less the pellucid structures of symbolic logic, but the language of everyday life. At that time he compiled a dictionary for use in primary schools. He found it a serious problem to maintain order in the class; he had himself to appear before the local magistrate on account of the corporal punishment of one of the pupils. Because of this and other difficulties he resigned from teaching. For some time after this he worked as a gardener in a monastery and helped as an architect in building a house for his sister.

Although Wittgenstein often discussed philosophy with friends who happened to call on him, such as F. P. Ramsey, Schlick and Waismann (a member of the Vienna Circle and later a philosophy don at Oxford), his philosophical interest was revived only when in the spring of 1928 he went with Waismann to hear a lecture by the Dutch mathematician L. E. J. Brouwer. Brouwer's conception of the foundations of mathematics held exciting implications for Wittgenstein even in the field of logic. He was persuaded to come to Cambridge, in the beginning of 1929, where he had many discussions with F. P. Ramsey, himself a mathematician. He spent several vacations in Vienna where he was able to talk with Waismann and Schlick. At the same time he was working on a book entitled *Philosophische Bemerkungen*, which, though handed in manuscript form to Moore in 1930, was not published until 1964.

Thus Wittgenstein resumed his philosophizing. In 1930 he became a fellow of Trinity College, Cambridge. In 1939 he was appointed Moore's successor, Moore having retired in that year. Around 1933 he began to circulate his new ideas in the form of two collections of lecture notes, the one in a blue folder, the other in a brown. They had a considerable effect. They were published after his death as *The Blue and Brown Books* (the only manuscript without a German original). He turns here to the study of ordinary language and instead of taking one use of language as ideal, the logical one, he begins to distinguish many uses.

At the outbreak of the Second World War Wittgenstein again left his work to take a job in a London hospital and later in a medical laboratory in Newcastle. He had obtained British nationality shortly after his arrival in England and he wanted to play a more active role in war-time than was possible within the walls of the ancient university. After the war he returned to Cambridge, but the prospect of resuming his professorship was somewhat abhorrent to him. Indeed, he found the whole atmosphere in Cambridge uncongenial. As a rule he took meals in his own room, rather than with other fellows at high table, because, as they said, he preferred not to wear a tie. When he had given a lecture he found himself always in such an excitable state that he would often go directly to a cinema. Only by immersing himself in a film could he forget his philosophizing. Finally, he discontinued his public lectures and confined his teaching to the small circle of a seminar—here at least he could do his thinking aloud.

At the end of 1947 Wittgenstein retired prematurely and was succeeded by one of his pupils, the Finn G. H. von Wright, who later, in 1954, having returned to Finland, wrote a biography of Wittgenstein, from which much material has been used in this chapter (see Biographical Sketch, in *Ludwig Wittgenstein: A Memoir* by Norman Malcolm, Oxford University Press). After his retirement he led a somewhat lonely and nomadic existence. He lived for a while in Ireland, Wales and Norway. He was attracted by rugged landscape, restless sea and hard-working fishermen. In the last years of his life he suffered from cancer. He continued even then to work out his new philosophy. His reflections from about 1936 to 1951 have been recorded in two later publications which in many places run parallel: *Philosophical Investigations*, published in 1953, devoted largely to the study of ordinary language, and *Remarks on the Foundations of Mathematics*, published in 1956, and concerned largely with artificial languages (logic, mathematics). The latter work, however, consists of notes which, in this form, Wittgenstein had not intended for publication. Both works appeared with German and English texts. In Germany his works are now being published with German text only. There are, finally, published notes of lectures by Wittgenstein (taken down by Moore) and of some lectures on ethics and other subjects (see Bibliography).

The last days of his life, in which he was seized with a zest for work, were spent at the home of his friend and physician, Dr. Bevan of Cambridge. There he died on April 29th 1951, three days after his 62nd birthday.

Just as his first main work was of great significance for logical positivism, so the works of his later period have been important for the movement known as linguistic analysis or analytical philosophy. The logical investigation of language is no less important here, but its purpose is to discover the different uses of language that are operative in everyday life. One is then led to consider not only logical structures but also, and more especially, patterns of human life. The view shifts from clear, almost timeless, logical rules to the variegated, historical manifestations of concrete life. It is important too that language is no longer conceived as a means of description merely, but also as an instrument of action, in which questions which originally were considered meaningless are now, within the field of linguistic analysis, fully allowed. These questions are not so far removed from those that are raised in traditional philosophy. Analytical philosophy, of which Austin, Ryle and Wisdom may be considered representatives, is still in process of development and receives much of its inspiration from the posthumous publications of Wittgenstein.

Wittgenstein has often been called a logician and a mystic. Both are present, though clearly distinguishable, in the *Tractatus* and in the *Notebooks* that prepared the way for the *Tractatus*—this will be shown in the two following chapters. In the later works these roles begin to merge. Yet the mystical strain of his thought never quite comes to the surface, and precisely because, according to Wittgenstein, this *cannot* be expressed in language. As a silent background to his philosophical activity it is highly significant for the understanding of the man and his work. His biographers—besides the one we have mentioned, a number of friends have written about him in various periodicals—have much to say on this point. We need only mention that Wittgenstein read a good deal of writers like Tolstoy and Dostoievsky. It was the harshness and idealism of their works that appealed to him rather than any philosophical reflections. In a letter to Malcolm (in 1945) he wrote, characteristically, that the philosophy of Tolstoy was most true when latent in the story. In his later work the meaning implied in an account of events becomes central for Wittgenstein.

Wittgenstein also began to read the Gospels and immersed himself in the work of Augustine and Kierkegaard. Augustine's best-known work '*The Confessions*' takes the form of a prayer.

Wittgenstein's works, and in particular the later ones, record his 'thinking aloud'. Certainly, there is a similarity in form between Augustine and Wittgenstein. Are there any further similarities? While they do share a concern for language and meaning, their respective conceptions of these are quite different. Yet there is in Wittgenstein a deeper, religious intention that brings him close to Augustine. In his foreword to *Philosophische Bermerkungen*, which carries a motto borrowed from Augustine, Wittgenstein says that he has written this book in good faith, that is to say—even though this would be misunderstood—'to the glory of God'.

In a letter to a friend Wittgenstein seemed to suggest that what he himself had been trying to say had already been said by Kierkegaard (in his emphasis on the individual's relation to God in the life of tension and paradox).

The mystical cannot be expressed in language—thus Wittgenstein in the *Tractatus*. In 1929 he said in a lecture on ethics, 'I can well imagine a religion in which there are no doctrines, in which therefore nothing is spoken.' In his later work language becomes more elastic and more comprehensive, though not in the form of theories or descriptions. Theology then is a question of 'grammar'; by this he means that it is only by knowing the rules of language and their applications that we can establish what theology is about. This idea has proved to be of use for certain American theologians, but was never worked out by Wittgenstein himself. For him, philosophy becomes more and more an activity which has first of all a practical, rather than logical or theoretical, purpose: learning to 'see'—a word he often used—the nature of human problems. He remained a 'positivist' in so far as he wished to avoid the errors of metaphysics and confine his attention to what is 'given' in language and thought, even though, as we shall see, he had no wish to deny a dimension of depth.

The theme of Wittgenstein's work is the question of 'meaning'. What is the meaning of a word and on what is it based? These are old philosophical questions, which have been discussed always in connection with problems of the relation between 'discourse' and 'truth' and in particular between 'thought' and 'being'. It is therefore not surprising that Wittgenstein preferred to read classical philosophers such as Plato and Augustine, who occupied themselves with just these questions of the meaning of words and concepts. Their solution, however, was not one that Wittgenstein could accept, and precisely for the reason that it was metaphysical. Wittgenstein was in many respects a self-taught philosopher and it is difficult to know which thinkers precisely had an influence on him. Certainly, Austrian philosophy and, more generally, mid-European philosophy played some part in shaping his thought. We have already mentioned that one of the books he read at school was by a pupil of Meinong. Meinong had corresponded with Russell and Moore, among others, on the subject of meanings. For each meaningful expression, according to him, there must be 'something' to which it corresponds and to which it points. This Meinong called the *Gegenstand* or 'object', though this was to be understood not as a material object, but as an object, for example, of imagination, of an untrue judgment, or of a wish. The term *Gegenstand* is also used by Wittgenstein in the sense of that to which the meaning of a name refers, as will be shown in the following chapter. Nevertheless, on a great number of points he disagrees with Meinong, even though some of his analyses bear a similarity to Meinong's, as for example his analysis of 'fact' (*Tatsache*). Meinong believed—and with him a number of other thinkers who had influenced Wittgenstein, such as the mathematician Frege in Germany and the philosophers Moore and Russell in England—that a meaningful expression names or points to something. This idea Wittgenstein rejected: a meaningful word is not a kind of name, its meaning is bound up with certain rules for the use of that word. Thus a meaningful word does not have to stand for something else, as the nameplate on a door refers to the occupant. To what, we might ask, do such words as 'centaur', 'pure equilateral triangle', 'not round' refer? Frege taught a kind of Platonism of meanings, that is to say that they corresponded to a higher realm of objects or entities which may often not be found in the world.

There is a further point. Two different words may sometimes have reference to the same object. By 'morning star' and 'evening star' we refer to the one planet Venus. Here Frege saw a distinction between the sense or '*Sinn*' and the reference or '*Bedeutung*'. In the example given the meanings in the first sense are different, while the meanings in the second sense are the same. This distinction reappears in Wittgenstein, who gives the word '*Sinn*' a logical definition which is related to the logical use one can make of a statement.

A line runs back from Frege and various Austrian philosophers (Meinong and Brentano, who taught both Meinong and Husserl), through Bolzano (1781–1848), a philosopher preoccupied with logical studies, to the great philosopher Leibniz (1646–1716). Leibniz had already tried to devise an all-embracing logic. His logical outlook pervaded his metaphysics: the factual and thus (often) the contingent and unintelligible, must ultimately be rooted in logical truth. By 'logical' here Leibniz means in accordance with the principle that within a given system no contradiction is possible (A is not non-A). The existence of God is the source of all non-contradiction. 'Why does this world exist?' 'Is the fact of the world's existence beyond explanation?' Such questions are intimately connected, for Leibniz, with the question of God's existence. His picture of the world then is to some extent a logical one. The relations in which the smallest units of the world (monads) stand to one another are purely logical, and in no sense external, spatial or physical; they are expressible in logical signs and they constitute necessarily, not merely contingently, the nature of these elements of the world.

This theme is also traceable in Wittgenstein, though any influence of Leibniz here is probably indirect. For example, Wittgenstein says in a lecture on ethics that there is a direct connection between the existence of the world and the existence of God. Considered in this light, statements of this kind become much more intelligible, as will be shown in Chapter Three. Moreover, the striking feature of Wittgenstein's picture of the world is that the basic elements that make up that world, referred to as 'objects' (*Gegenstand*), are logically defined and not conceived as accidental and contingent facts, as will appear in the following chapter. Where he differs from Leibniz and from the Dutch philosopher Spinoza (1632–1677), who in this respect stands behind him, is that for him the facticity of the world can no longer be illuminated by, or logically derived from, the existence of God. It is precisely this, the existence of God, which cannot be said or logically thought, even though Wittgenstein appears in the *Tractatus* to be familiar with certain Spinozan terms. The logical reduction and the mystical vision 'in the light of eternity', which form one perspective in Spinoza, are for Wittgenstein two different dimensions, the one of that which can logically be said, the other of that which proves to be unsayable.

The same might be said even more fittingly in the case of Schopenhauer's philosophy, with which, as we have noted, Wittgenstein was acquainted. Schopenhauer (1788–1860) was in a sense both an advocate and an opponent of Leibniz's ideas, although it should also be said that between these philosophers —in a more than chronological sense—there stands that great philosopher Kant. One fundamental problem he shared with Leibniz was the problem of accounting for the factual world. He often made use of a basic rule of thought which had been established by Leibniz but which for Schopenhauer was a strictly logical rule, namely that of 'sufficient reason'. According to this rule, there must be a sufficient explanation for every factual event. He agreed with Kant, as against Leibniz, in maintaining that the laws in terms of which we can explain natural events do not reside in nature itself, but derive from the disposition of our minds. Strictly there are no natural laws, but only the law-like regularities and forms of our own conceptual powers. Again, as to the metaphysical question of the meaning of the world, Schopenhauer departed from Leibniz by developing a pessimistic philosophy. For Schopenhauer the world first becomes a problem at the practical, not at the theoretical, level. The question is not so much, 'why does the world exist?' but 'why must it exist?' This question does not arise from our understanding or rational capacities, but from our irrational will. He was also concerned with the questions of happiness and of immortality, which for him—as for Kant in another respect—are closely related to our will. 'World' is connected with 'Life'. Our conceptual world, the world of science and theory in which man is a mere object (a body), is limited and determined by our own forms of knowledge. The more profound, authentic reality lies behind this, in the non-conceptual active will, in which man, far from being an object, is an irrational subject, an 'I'.

Wittgenstein, as will appear, also distinguishes between the world as idea (objective, logically structured) and as will (inexpressible, the will being related to 'I'). The metaphysical questions of happiness and immortality, which certainly have a place in his thought, are tackled from the point of view of an analysis and critique of language. This had already been done by F. Mauthner (whom Wittgenstein had read) in, for example, the critique of language he published at the beginning of the century. Language, according to Mauthner, is a defective tool for acquiring knowledge, a ladder one must throw away after use—the phrase recurs in Wittgenstein. If Schopenhauer was looking for some ultimate explanation of the world and believed he had found it in the 'will', he was misled by the abstractions of language. Even talk of an irrational 'I' is meaningless, adds nothing to our knowledge, because it is an emotional cry, a 'babbling tautology', in which one can only say, 'I,I,I'. A logic of the facts is impossible and also what is known as 'measuring' is not based on something in the nature of things, but refers only to a measure that is set up by man.

Similarly Wittgenstein rejects any 'logic of the facts', brings a language critique to bear on metaphysics, and even considers talk of the 'I' to be impossible. But he dissents from Mauthner when he sets a positive value on such critique of language and hopes by means of it to arrive at a logical system of measurement. At this point he was influenced from other directions: in particular, by positivist-minded thinkers who wished to combine empirically controllable elements within a logically ordered language. Among these was Ernst Mach, who exercised a considerable influence on the group which developed into the Vienna Circle—there was also in Vienna an 'Ernst Mach Society'. One of his works he dedicated to Karl Pearson, who had written a book at the end of the previous century under the title *The Grammar of Science*. It was also Wittgenstein's intention to begin with positive elements and to produce a kind of 'grammar' of scientific thought. He discovered such a grammar in some of the natural sciences and he is known to have had in mind, in the writing of the *Tractatus*, a textbook on mechanics by Marcus Hertz. We must further note the influence of an entirely different thinker, G. C. Lichtenberg (eighteenth century), who wrote in a witty and often obscure aphoristic style. He maintained that the whole of philosophy was nothing more than criticism of the uses of language.

Wittgenstein's contact with the above-mentioned positivists

on the one hand, and with those on the other hand who were concerned with the foundations of logic and mathematics, such as Frege, Russell and Whitehead, was of the greatest significance for the development of his ideas on language and thought. We can see their influence in other respects. Russell and Whitehead both held a dynamic, rather than static, view of reality, in so far as they thought of reality as made up of certain basic 'events'. Wittgenstein was to speak later of 'states of affairs' as constituting the world, but for him they acquire their connectedness only by virtue of language, which relates one to another. Russell taught further that logical language reflected these elements of the world. These elements he also called 'atoms', though he wished to make it clear that these were to be understood as logical and not physical 'atoms', i.e., as such logically definable elements as relations and colour-patches. Wittgenstein propounds this logical atomism in the *Tractatus*, but in his delineation of the logical structure of the world he goes further than Russell, showing, for example, not that there are such empirical entities as coloured patches, but that a patch must, logically, have *some* colour or other. Russell is closer than Wittgenstein to the tradition of British empiricism.

There is an analogous difference between Wittgenstein, in his later phase, and G. E. Moore (1873–1958). Moore defends realism—belief in the existence of the external world—by a careful and often linguistic analysis of concepts, which has much in common with the method Wittgenstein employed in the later phase. We have noted that the two men often met for discussion. Moore, however, appeals to 'common sense', and this sober, empirical kind of argument Wittgenstein finds superficial. He pleads rather for 'depth grammar', that is to say, for a probing into the underlying rules that govern our thought and speech.

The enumeration of thinkers who might have influenced Wittgenstein is not our greatest concern, however. It is to see how Wittgenstein, in his own, original way, tackled the age-old problems of philosophy. How do words and thoughts acquire their *meaning*? How does our thought find its way through the labyrinth of words?

CHAPTER TWO

The Logic of Speech

'1   The world is all that is the case.

1·1   The world is the totality of facts, not of things.

1·11   The world is determined by the facts, and by their being all the facts.

1·12   For the totality of facts determines what is the case, and also whatever is not the case.

1·13   The facts in logical space are the world.

1·2   The world divides into facts.

1·21   Each item can be the case or not the case while everything else remains the same.

2   What is the case—a fact—is the existence of states of affairs.

2·01   A state of affairs (a state of things) is a combination of objects (things).

2·011   It is essential to things that they should be possible constituents of states of affairs.

2·012   In logic nothing is accidental: if a thing can occur in a state of affairs, the possibility of the state of affairs must be written into the thing itself.

2·014   Objects contain the possibility of all situations.

2·0141   The possibility of its occurring in states of affairs is the form of an object.

2·02   Objects are simple.

2·0201   Every statement about complexes can be resolved into a statement about their constituents and into the propositions that describe the complexes completely.

2·021　Objects make up the substance of the world. That is why they cannot be composite.

2·1　We picture facts to ourselves.

2·11　A picture presents a situation in logical space, the existence and non-existence of states of affairs.

2·12　A picture is a model of reality.

2·13　In a picture objects have the elements of the picture corresponding to them.

2·131　In a picture the elements of the picture are representatives of objects.

2·14　What constitutes a picture is that its elements are related to one another in a determinate way.'

THESE quotations from the beginning of the *Tractatus* present features that are characteristic of all Wittgenstein's thinking. The decimal numbering is particularly striking. It was used by Russell and Whitehead (in *Principia Mathematica*) rather as a scheme of classification. It indicates the level of argumentation. Propositions such as 1, 2 and 3 are on one level; 1·1 and 2·1 are further specified and are thus on a different level. Besides switching from one level to another, one can also ramify the argument on one level (e.g. 1·11, 1·12), or jump a level, as it were, by setting out immediately the finer points of a thesis (e.g. 2, 2·01, 2·02). The book contains seven main points. The first, as can be seen above, is dealt with very briefly. The second takes about five pages, the third about ten pages, the fourth, fifth and sixth fifteen to twenty-five each, while the seventh consists of one sentence. Those dealt with most fully largely concern matters of symbolic logic. The shorter expositions concern the relation of logical language to reality.

The opening theses of the book present Wittgenstein's theory of the world, his 'ontology', one might say. At this point, how ever, some commentators raise a question. When he talks of the 'world', is he in fact talking of reality (ontology), or is he rather talking of the language world? Are not these opening theses to be taken as recommendations to use certain terms, like 'world' and 'fact', in a certain way? The point of these questions is to suggest not that Wittgenstein might not be presenting an ontology but that he wants to set problems of ontology and epistemology immediately in the context of logic. Thus, as early as 1·13 he uses the expression 'logical space'. This becomes clearer if we read him backwards, and then note how his 'ontology' prepares the way for his analysis of the logical structure of language. 'The totality of propositions is language' (4·001). 'In a proposition a thought finds an expression that can be perceived by the senses' (3·1). 'A logical picture of facts is a thought' (3). 'We picture facts to ourselves' (2·1). 'The world is the totality of facts, not of things' (1·1). The last thesis is almost isomorphic with the first, linguistic thesis (4·001) and forms its ontological counterpart. The intermediate steps are: proposition, thought, logical picture, picture in general, facts. These bridge the gulf between language (and thought) and the world.

If we now read the theses in their proper order, we see that they all refer to one structure: there is one logical space for what can be called 'the world', 'thought' and 'language'. 'The limits of my language mean the limits of my world. Logic pervades the world: the limits of the world are also its limits' (5·6 and 5·61). This implies that one can never adopt a position outside logical space and then speak *about* the structure, about language as a whole or about the correspondence between language and the world. Because of this the problems of ontology, as we said above, are placed at the outset in the context of logic. The questions raised in the classical theory of knowledge as to the link between knowledge and reality, the operation of the world on consciousness and *vice versa*, are ruled out of order. The ontological theses—those that deal with 'the world' and 'facts'—are so much part of the whole logical structure of the *Tractatus*, so determined by it, that they directly entail the correspondence between language (thought) and the world (reality). An additional theory about this correspondence is superfluous, or, to speak more precisely, impossible.

The ontological theses entail, very generally, two theses concerning the correspondence between language and the world. First, that the logical structure of language sets the bounds to what can possibly occur in the world. Secondly, that whether an event actually does occur has to be decided a case at a time— verification. The theses 1·13 and 1·2 anticipate these two sorts of correspondence: the global and structural (to be linked, as we shall see, with 'logical meaning'), and the factual (to be linked with 'referential meaning'). How the two are related will become clear when we consider how facts are constructed from states of affairs and how states of affairs are understood as a connection of 'things' or 'objects'.

To explain all this we shall have to consider the following themes: 'facts' are not things, not even physical atoms, for they are constructed from states of affairs (p. 34); 'the world', as a term, comprises both isolated facts and the whole range of logically conceivable relations between facts (p. 35), by which Wittgenstein does *not* mean physical relations, such as causality —he is concerned with possible relations, with the 'how' not the 'that' (pp. 56–8); the negation of a proposition does not give a different meaning to the proposition, but a different logical form; the negation of a proposition is not the same as its falsity (pp. 36–40); the term 'world', as encompassing 'all the facts', implies the concept of a 'limit'—the limitedness of the world and of language is something which 'shows' itself, and the importance of this will be seen in the more metaphysical theses with which Wittgenstein closes his book (pp. 41–6).

In the opening theses we are offered a picture of the world as made up, not of elements or things, but of facts—it is accordingly a non-substantialist picture of the world. A fact is what is the case. A fact, it appears later, is indispensable for the verification of a proposition. To talk of a 'fact' is to say that there must be something in the world in terms of which language, i.e. propositions, can be true or false, for language can be compared with reality (4·05) and this function of language as a 'picture' contains the possibility of its being true or false (4·06).

'What is the case—a fact—is the existence of states of affairs' (2). Wittgenstein uses the term '*Sachverhalt*'; a fact is a complex of states of affairs which correspond to elementary propositions: the single fact that there is a chair here is, as it were, a junction of innumerable states of affairs, for instance, that the chair is standing on the floor, that it is behind the table, that it is brown, that it is a wooden chair, etc. These states of affairs do not and cannot exist in isolation or, so to speak, in themselves. They are aspects of the fact, and can be formulated in logical language; they are the possibilities which are realized and actualized in an existing fact. The term '*Sachverhalt*', rendered in the first and second translations as, respectively, 'atomic fact' and 'state of affairs', is one of the key terms of the *Tractatus*. It refers indeed to the 'atoms' from which, logically speaking, the world is constructed. The term 'atomic fact' recalls the logical atomism of Russell, which carries over into Wittgenstein's ontology. Originally Wittgenstein spoke also of 'atomic propositions', which correspond to 'atomic facts', and it is therefore not surprising that Wittgenstein should have approved this translation of *Sachverhalt*. But this is not to say that the logical atom is a static element or substance, for it contains the idea that something is the case, that the presence or absence of a certain state of affairs can be established—in the new translation of *Sachverhalt* as 'state of affairs' this is taken into account. Thus the world is not the totality of things, such as glasses and tables, but rather of states of affairs, such as this glass being on the table.

States of affairs must each be expressed by a sentence, not by a word—hence Wittgenstein's proposition-logic. On the other hand, these states of affairs, and the facts in which they occur, are quite detached from one another: 'The world divides into facts' (1·2). A state of affairs implies a constellation, a relation. Etymologically, the German word suggests a 'hold of things', as Miss Anscombe has noted. It is relations that are first given, not things. Things make their appearance only within a space of possible states of affairs, as in the case where the speck that is red is one of the possible states of affairs—it could have been yellow or green as well—in which a speck must necessarily occur.

Such states of affairs—the glass is on the table, it is raining outside, John is hitting Peter, etc.—are connections of 'objects'. The word 'object'—in the German, '*Gegenstand*'—is meant to indicate whatever can be given as a datum, activities and qualities as well as things. Both Whitehead and Russell had spoken of 'events', as certain occurrences in a situation or constellation. Such data as glasses, tables, raindrops, John, are mere abstractions by themselves, for what is given in reality is not separate entities, but actual relations and events. Objects have a logical character for Wittgenstein—he is *not* talking of physical objects —and what this means precisely will be explained later on. In any case, it should be clear by now that Wittgenstein's concern is not merely with a doctrine of events or of states of affairs. He wants to elucidate the logical structure of the world. He therefore tries to present states of affairs or, as he also says, the connection of objects, in the form of a logical language. Just as in geometry it is possible to project objects on a plane, so a particular event or state of affairs can be projected in a logical picture. This is done by showing that certain logical elements are mutually related in a certain way. That the glass is on the table, for example, can be expressed in logical terms as '*a R b*', where '*a*' and '*b*' indicate things and '*R*' indicates a relation. It is this kind of connection that indicates the facts within what Wittgenstein calls logical space. Logical space covers the field of the possible relations that may obtain between states of affairs, and that are realized in positive facts. 'The glass is on the table' is an indication of such a positive fact, translatable in logical language as '*a R b*' or in terms of signs representing whole sentences (atomic propositions), as '*p*'. These sentences, or, to use the more technical term, these 'propositions', may occur in extensive constellations. For example, 'The glass is on the table and the clock is on the wall' would be rendered '*p & q*'; 'It is always raining here or it is cold' would be '*p* v *q*'. The first constellation is called a 'conjunction' and is known as a logical product. The second is a 'disjunction'—the use of the word 'or' does not preclude the possibility that both *p* and *q* are valid, that, in the example given, it is both raining and cold—and it is known as a logical sum.

Wittgenstein distinguishes elementary propositions, such as '*p*' and '*q*', from the complex propositions that are constructed from them, such as '*p & q*' and '*p* v *q*'. The first he calls pictures of reality, though he speaks of them also as models, which suggests they are something other than direct representations. He gives the example of a fencing lesson, in which the teacher shows by means of a little doll which moves it would be wrong to make. In logic one can show by a proposition what is not the case. One can place a negation sign in front of a proposition: '~*p*', signifying e.g. 'It is not raining.' But how can one portray in language that something is not the case in reality? This question was fundamental for Wittgenstein. (It appeared to him eventually to be an essentially metaphysical question.) If I write down '*p*', I can also, by a simple operation, write down the negation, '~*p*'. Indeed, '*p*' and '~*p*' are so directly related to one another, so to speak, that when I affirm a state of affairs in a proposition (e.g. 'it is raining'), I indicate at the same time the area outside this state of affairs which is contained in the negation of the state of affairs. In a given proposition, 'p', I indicate one point within logical space, and in the negation of this proposition, '$\sim p$', I indicate whatever falls outside it. Thus Wittgenstein can say that the denial of a proposition—the logical operation called negation ('$\sim$')—refers to the logical place indicated by the affirming proposition (p), but that the negating proposition itself ($\sim p$) indicates *another* logical place, namely, that which lies outside the state of affairs indicated by 'p' (4·0641). In a letter to Russell (19th August 1919) Wittgenstein argues that negative propositions are never elementary. In the first instance a statement affirms something; it is a projection in language of a state of affairs; it is a positive picture. Wittgenstein had tackled this problem in his *Notebooks* of 1914–1917: 'that shadow which the picture as it were casts upon the world: How am I to get an exact grasp of it? Here is a deep mystery. It is the mystery of negation: This is not how things are, and yet we can say *how* things are *not*' (p. 30).

Something can be the case or not be the case. States of affairs are not necessary, for they could be otherwise. That something is the case is not logically necessary or logically demonstrable, for it could also not be the case. This characteristic of states of affairs—that they only 'happen' to exist—is known as contingency. That something actually occurs (that, e.g., the glass is on the table) is a contingent fact and every proposition, in referring to reality, is itself contingent, which is to say that it can be either true or false. The terms 'true' and 'false' are sharply distinguished by Wittgenstein from affirmation and negation. It is not the case that 'p' signifies that a certain state of affairs is true, while '$\sim p$' says that a state of affairs is in reality false. For one cannot know, merely by looking at a projected picture, a model, a series of connected signs, whether something is true in reality. This is evident from the fact that 'p' can be either true or false, that someone may say, for example, 'it is raining' when in reality it is not raining. So too '$\sim p$' can be either true or false. To be sure, Frege, Russell and Whitehead made use of the sign '⊢' to determine that a proposition is true (e.g. '⊢p'), but Wittgenstein rejected this notation for the reason that no proposition of itself can ever say whether it is true or false. It is not logically contradictory to write after 'p' '$\sim p$'. It is evident that the possibility that something does not exist or does not occur can nevertheless be presented in language—by a sign of negation. Thus the logical problem of how something can *not* be the case is answered by Wittgenstein in terms of a linguistic operation negating a positive assertion: '$\sim p$'. In tackling this question, which he does repeatedly, Wittgenstein is touching on an old metaphysical problem, namely, how is one to relate the logically necessary (the logical structure of language, thought and the world) to the contingent (factual existence)? How is one to relate the 'how' to the 'that'?

It should be clear in what follows that the questions that occurred to him at this early stage governed the whole development of his thought. At this point, however, it is worth noting that he was discussing problems that had already been tackled in various ways by Frege, Meinong, Russell, Husserl and Moore. These philosophers were asking, for example, how a statement can be said to have meaning if, on the face of it, there is nothing in reality to correspond to such a statement. Wittgenstein, through the different phases of his thought, offered an increasingly subtle answer to the question. It is already clear from some notes on logic in 1913 that his views were at variance with those of Frege and Russell. Frege, as appeared in the previous chapter, distinguished between '*Sinn*' (logical meaning) and '*Bedeutung*' (referential meaning); but he believed that '*Sinn*' denoted something, because, to his mind, a proposition should be conceived as a name. Here Wittgenstein demurred. Propositions are not names, he says, still less names of compounds (cf. *Tractatus* 3·143, 5·02). His 'break-through' on the problem was to say that 'p' has the same meaning as '$\sim p$', that the meaning of a proposition lies in its reference to a corresponding state of affairs.

This is to say that logical operations such as negation ('$\sim$', in ordinary language 'not'), conjunction ('&' 'and'), and disjunction ('v', 'or') do not themselves indicate anything in reality. 'My fundamental idea is that the "logical constants" are not representatives; that there can be no representatives of the *logic* of facts' (4·0312). It is the variable signs in logical notation which represent things and facts, not the logical constants such as '$\sim$' and '&'. Only for the variable signs in a proposition, signifying objects, does Wittgenstein use the term 'name'. The point at issue is the logical name-function of a sign—in ordinary language we may well use names to describe characteristics (as bearing 'connotation', not merely 'denotation'), as for example when we say, 'he speaks like Cicero'. 'A name means an object. The object is its meaning' (3·203). We may conclude that logical meaning is ascribed by Wittgenstein to the structure of the proposition, and thus to the logical network of language; the referential meaning of a proposition depends on those words within it that function as names and on the related possibility of the proposition pointing to states of affairs. Names have the value of merely indicating (denotation), not of describing (connotation). In Wittgenstein's later work the matter is different: words that function as names have now no well-defined object as their meaning, for what precisely do we mean by names like 'brown', 'red', 'Moses'? We must have a certain agreement about the rules which govern the use of such words (cf. *Philosophical Investigations*, pp. 36–9). With these less strictly limited, more flexible and more coherent rules of language there is also a loose denotation. This will be taken up again in the last two chapters.

The point can be made in another way. Complex propositions (e.g. 'p & q') can always be reduced to elementary propositions ('p', 'q'). And this applies equally to negation ('$\sim$'). Positive and negative propositions map out the area of logical space, though negation as such does not occur in reality. Wittgenstein's doctrine of negation contains an idea that can also be found in more metaphysical philosophers: the idea, namely, that negation and 'nothingness' are no part of what is given in the world, but are brought into the world by the spirit—thus Hegel and Sartre. This implies, what has already been said, that meaning (*Bedeutung*) lies in the reference of logical language to states of affairs, and that meaning is not to be thought of as something behind language which language in general 'names'. A negation, for example, is not a name for something in the world; it is rather an operation with signs, which thus offers no new experience, yet which does serve to order and elucidate our knowledge.

Wittgenstein speaks also of positive facts—the existence of states of affairs—and negative facts—the non-existence of states of affairs (2·06). However, this is not a matter of *logical* negation, but of the comparison of statements with reality. If a negative proposition ('$\sim p$') is verified, we may then talk of the non-existence of a state of affairs. This presupposes, however, that we know the referential meaning of the positive proposition ('p'), in the case of its being true. Wittgenstein had already made this point in his 'Notes on Logic' in 1913 (*Notebooks*, p. 94): 'There are positive and negative facts: if the proposition "This rose is not red" is true, then what it signifies is negative; but the occurrence of the word "not" does not indicate this unless we know that the signification of the proposition "This rose is red" (when it is true) is positive.' His answer to the question as to what exactly the negative proposition corresponds to—it was a question raised at the beginning of this century by many philosophers—is to say that negation as a logical operation has *no* referential meaning. Yet negation, as Wittgenstein puts it, casts a shadow on the world. For the case of a negative proposition being true can have reference to the world by way of the referential meaning of a true positive proposition, so that one can indeed talk of negative facts. Logical space (the logical possibilities or structure), together with everything that is the case and is not the case (1·12 and 2·06), mark out the boundaries of reality. Wittgenstein provides an illustration of this in his 'Notes on Logic' (*Notebooks*, p. 95): 'The comparison of language and reality is like that of a retinal image and visual image: to the blind spot nothing in the visual image seems to correspond, and thereby the boundaries of the blind spot determine the visual image—just as true negations of atomic propositions determine reality.' So negation, as something that belongs to the logical form (the 'how'), together with the property 'true', as something that belongs to facticity (the 'that'), can indicate the boundary of the world. The concept of the 'boundary' will turn out to be important for Wittgenstein.

If a proposition is not compared with factual reality, one cannot say whether it is true or false. Propositions may well display, in their mutual relations, a clear logical behaviour which makes it possible for the terms 'true' and 'false' to be applied to them. Thus it is clear that if 'p' is true, then '$\sim p$' cannot also be true at the same time. In all this, however, nothing has been said about reality, for it is quite possible in this case that 'p' is false and that, accordingly, '$\sim p$' is true. What has been said concerns logic: one can formulate a logical axiom in the form, '$\sim(p \,\&\, \sim p)$', which negates the simultaneous validity of p and not-p. If it is assumed that 'p' can be either true or false, then both cases can be applied to the sign 'p' (as a variable). It will then be found that, in virtue of the relations determined by the logical constants, '$\sim$' and '&', and also by the puntuation mark, '( )', the composite proposition as a whole can only be true.

This example, quite obviously, is an exceptional case, for most propositions, whether simple or complex, are either true or false. This is most clearly seen with regard to the complex proposition, because, as Wittgenstein puts it, it is a truth-function of elementary propositions. That is to say, it is true or false according to the truth and falsity of the propositions of which it is composed. To explain how this was so Wittgenstein drew up some 'truth-tables'—they have since been taken over by modern logic. For example, the complex proposition '$p \vee q$' would be determined by the following table:

p q	$p \vee q$
T T	T
T F	T
F T	T
F F	F

In this table the truth ('T') or falsity ('F') of the full sentence, '$p \vee q$', depends on whether the separate statements, 'p' and 'q', are themselves true or false. It then appears that by the logical disjunction ('$\vee$') we are to understand that combination of separate judgments that would be true if both judgments are true, or if either one of them is true, and false if both judgments are false. Hence: $TTTF$. Conjunction (p and q, or 'p & q') would similarly yield the following: $TFFF$.

As we have already seen, certain combinations are possible which always yield the truth-value 'true', and certain others which always yield 'false'. It is not always very obvious that a given complex proposition is invariably true or, to use the technical term, a tautology, nor, on the other hand, that a given proposition is invariably false, that is to say, contradictory. The point of a truth-table is to make this clear. A tautology can be thought of as a border-line case among other propositions which are sometimes true, sometimes false. Wittgenstein even speaks of it as a 'degenerate' complex proposition, since it can only be true and since it is in no way contingent upon factual states of affairs and therefore no way informative. If one were to say for example that it is raining or it is not raining ('p v $\sim p$'), this would indeed be true, but it would tell us nothing about the weather.

A tautology is further described as 'senseless'. He does not mean to say that such a proposition is nonsensical. On the contrary, it may be of great importance. Kant's problem of how pure mathematics is possible—a true and conclusive doctrine of relations, independent of actual events—is now solved, so Wittgenstein claimed as early as 1914. One can never say beforehand of actual, and thus contingent, events that they *must* be the case, but statements of mathematics and logic do not share in the uncertainties of reality and are therefore always valid. Now, according to Wittgenstein, logical laws are tautologies, complex statements which can only be true. It is for this reason that the propositions of logic are necessary and indubitable; but in fact they tell us nothing. 'Hence there can *never* be surprises in logic' (6·1251). Logic is anything but nonsensical, for it is a means for gaining clarification. And yet it provides no new experience, no additional information about the world.

If logic is such an illuminating structure of relations, and valid independently of the facts, why then should it be described as 'senseless'? The answer to this is that the strength of a tautology is at the same time its weakness: a tautology has *no* truth-conditions, since it is unconditionally true (4·461). Now Wittgenstein defines the term 'sense'—the sense of a proposition—as the possibility of a statement having truth-conditions, that is, the possibility of agreeing with the existence and non-existence of states of affairs (4·2). This use of the word 'sense' ('*Sinn*'), which makes it equivalent to 'logical meaning', should be distinguished from what Wittgenstein calls *'Bedeutung'* ('referential meaning': the reference of, e.g., '*p*' and '$\sim p$' to the same state of affairs). By 'sense' we are to understand a meaning that lies in the logical apparatus itself, a meaning ascribed to a statement when it is capable of being true or false. It is not the case that '*p*' is true and '$\sim p$' false, but both, as we have seen, must be either true or false, and accordingly in complex propositions their mutual relation is such that if one is true the other is false. This then is a tautology or logical law, but in saying this we have presupposed that the individual sentences have a logical meaning or sense, that they can, in other words, be true or false, correct or incorrect pictures of reality. More broadly speaking, for a statement to be meaningful it must be clear that reality can be compared with the statement. The affirmation and the negation of a proposition (e.g. '*p*' and '$\sim p$') affirm and negate the *sense* which the proposition already has—the expression 'it is raining' must first have sense, be applicable to some state of affairs, be capable of being true or false, before one can formulate the logical affirmation or negation, 'it is raining' or 'it is not raining' (cf. 4·05–4·064).

Here we meet some of the fundamental difficulties of Wittgenstein's logical atomism. First of all, it is clear from what has been said that logical constants never indicate whether a proposition is in fact true or false. Their meaning is not that they stand for something in reality, but lies entirely in the rules that arise in their mutual relations. They have no referential meaning (*Bedeutung*), but a logical meaning (*Sinn*), which consists of the possibility of being sometimes true and sometimes false. Thus one may calculate by means of a truth-table that the proposition '$\sim (p \vee q)$' can be converted, purely on the basis of the rules, into '$\sim p \,\&\, \sim q$', since both prove to yield the same truth-conditions: *FFFT*. However, that one case will in fact occur—that, for example, it will so happen that at a certain time it will be raining and yet not be cold—which will prove the proposition symbolized as '$\sim p$ & $\sim q$' to be entirely false (where 'p' stands for 'it is raining' and 'q' for 'it is cold'), is something which can never be shown in the logical symbolism of the proposition. Logic and language are unable to express their own factual agreement with reality. What they do show is that statements *can* be true or false.

This last point bears on the distinction Wittgenstein makes between 'saying' and 'showing', as in his statement 'What can be shown cannot be said' (4·1212). The various implications of this idea will be pointed out later—in particular, that it is impossible to talk *about* language and logical structures. First, however, we need an outline of the general problem of 'saying' and 'showing', and especially because Wittgenstein himself, in a letter to Russell (19th August 1919), called this 'the cardinal problem of philosophy'. If we wish to discover whether a proposition is true, we need first to understand the proposition, which means 'to know what is the case if it is true' (4·024). Now this cannot be *said*, for it is a condition of our being able to say something (we must know the logical structure, the sense, of a proposition before we can actually use it in language). So Wittgenstein says, 'A proposition *shows* its sense' (4·022). What it 'shows', however, is not merely the material aspect of the sense, so that we can anticipate that the proposition could in fact be true, but also, more broadly, its formal aspect. Wittgenstein speaks of 'the logical form, i.e. the form of reality' (2·18) and makes the point that 'a picture cannot . . . depict its pictorial form: it displays it' (2·172). As we discovered earlier in connection with the negation sign, a logical form implies ultimately the limitation of the whole of logical space and, further, as we shall see more clearly in the following chapter, these 'limits of the world' cannot be said, they can only be shown.

We might appreciate the distinction better if we noted, first, that philosophy for Wittgenstein is in the end a more practical affair than pure theory, mere talk, could ever be: 'Philosophy is not a theory but an activity.' The 'showing' is concerned above all with the *rules* of linguistic use, which is to say already that its function is practical—in Wittgenstein's later work it was to become more central and, to a certain extent, even sayable.

The second point relates this distinction to the rather curious 'ontology' referred to at the beginning of this chapter. Wittgenstein departs from the customary idea that a logical system comes into being by a choice of primitive (undefined) terms, symbols, axioms and rules of inference that is quite arbitrary, i.e. not informed by any 'ontological' or 'material' considerations. On this account one then proceeds to interpret the logical system in a particular way (one takes the initially formal symbols to represent something), for example, by setting up a model of the system (the model would include elements derived from the factual world). Finally, one discovers whether the model fits reality, by way of verification or falsification. For Wittgenstein an arbitrary choice of this kind is impossible, for one can frame an intelligible structure only if it agrees with the structure of reality. Language and propositions fall under the more general term 'picture'. And a picture of reality, whether it comes about through a combination of elements of language or of other things, as in the reconstruction of a car accident by means of small dolls and toy cars, is itself a model. 'A picture is a model of reality' (2·12). Here the model is not an interpretation of a formal system of symbols, but each system of symbols is already part of a 'picture' or 'model'. Thus a system is formal, for Wittgenstein, not because it is arbitrary, but because it represents possible, rather than factual, reality: 'Pictorial form is the possibility that things are related to one another in the same way as elements of the picture' (2·151). This helps to explain why an ontological discussion is actually impossible: language already presupposes its own model-character and so this cannot itself be discussed. Indeed, this whole representation of the structure of reality (the 'how') in language can no longer be said, it can only be shown.

The difficulty here is to know how it can be shown that a certain proposition corresponds, or fails to correspond, to the reality, that it is in fact true or false. A proposition as such has two truth-possibilities: it can be true or false. A complex proposition, 'p & q', has four truth-possibilities, as can be shown from the truth-table—p and q can both be T, p can be T and q F, p can be F and q T, p and q can both be F. With three propositions there are 2^3 or 8 possibilities, and so on. How is one to establish which of these actually occurs at a given moment? The answer is that one learns this, not from the symbolism or from language itself, but from testing the statement by reality. This is known as verification: the network of language with its many truth-possibilities is compared with reality, the reality being far more limited because only one of the possibilities will prove to be realized.

But what if such a test cannot in principle be carried out? In this case there are no truth-possibilities and the statement accordingly is void of sense. This idea has gained influence in logical positivism, where the requirement of verifiability has been laid down as a criterion for determining whether or not a statement is meaningful. Metaphysical statements, because they go beyond all empirical experience and are thus incapable of verification, count in logical positivism as meaningless language. But what can and what cannot be verified? A famous slogan of logical positivism, flourished by Schlick and Ayer among others, was: the meaning of a statement is the way in which it is verified. The statement has been ascribed to Wittgenstein, and Moore tells us that Wittgenstein had made use of it in his lectures, but that he added later that what precisely was meant by verification was difficult to define. Is it merely a question of empirical procedures? Would, for example, the procedures of psychology or history be included? In the *Tractatus* Wittgenstein gives an extremely concise and yet broad definition: 'To understand a proposition means to know what is the case if it is true' (4·024). In a later work he puts it as follows: 'The meaning of a question is the method of answering it'; 'every proposition is the direction for a verification' (*Philosophische Bemerkungen*, pp. 12, 174).

The second question that arises in this connection is whether it is possible to speak about logic and language. Can one express the agreement or disagreement of a statement with reality in the form of another statement? The second statement would also be governed by logical rules. There would then be a kind of meta-logic or at any rate a meta-language. Strictly speaking, the sign '⊢', used by Frege and others to posit the truth of a proposition, was already a piece of meta-language, because it *added* to the then existing logic the assertion that a particular statement agreed with the actual state of affairs. Various logicians, including Carnap, have attempted to construct a meta-language, but to Wittgenstein the project is impossible. Logic is a closed system, but it cannot of itself say that a certain statement is true —to be sure, the meaning of the statement rests on logic, as has already been said.

Logic must look after itself, writes Wittgenstein (5·473). For it in no way depends on a mystical intuition, by which one might discover a logical law in reality itself which is then transcribed in language. Logic is concerned with a series of operations, like negation and conjunction, which are seen to display a certain logical behaviour: there are connections and ultimately certain ground-rules by which one is able to convert or reduce one statement to another (e.g. '$\sim (p \vee q)$' to '$\sim p \,\&\, \sim q$'). The ground-rules that operate here are tautologies. That is to say, one can tell from the symbolism alone that they must always be true (e.g. '$p \vee \sim p$'). Beside these logically necessary propositions, which exemplify logical rules, there are contingent propositions which may or may not be true. These are characterized by the fact that their truth or falsity cannot be recognized from the propositions alone (6·113).

No room is left for a meta-language. There are merely, on the one hand, logical rules and the analysis of statements regardless of their factual truth or falsity, and on the other hand, there is the testing of a statement by a state of affairs, and for this one might be given at the most some practical directions, but never logical rules. Wittgenstein maintains that the testing of assertions by verification can lead only to physical statements, so that experiential judgments fall within the sphere of the natural sciences—here Wittgenstein is pointing to a more limited conception of verification. Philosophy has no sphere of its own that might exist beside or above the sphere of science. Philosophy is concerned with the logical analysis of language. As such it is to be described in functional rather than substantial terms, as being concerned with an activity rather than with an aspect or part of reality.

'4·11   The totality of true propositions is the whole of natural science (or the whole corpus of the natural sciences).

4·111   Philosophy is not one of the natural sciences. (The word "philosophy" must mean something whose place is above or below the natural sciences, not beside them.)

4·112   Philosophy aims at the logical clarification of thoughts. Philosophy is not a body of doctrines but an activity. A philosophical work consists essentially of elucidations. Philosophy does not result in "philosophical propositions", but rather in the clarification of propositions. Without philosophy thoughts are, as it were, cloudy and indistinct : its task is to make them clear and to give them sharp boundaries.'

THE LOGIC OF SPEECH

At the beginning of the *Tractatus*, which was quoted earlier, Wittgenstein speaks of the picture that we can form of reality and in which, by way of a model, we represent the existence and non-existence of states of affairs. It is in the possibility of agreeing or disagreeing with reality, thus being true or false, that the meaning of the picture lies (cf. 2·222). The same thought occurs later when Wittgenstein describes spoken and written language, i.e. propositions, as one of these pictures, and defines its meaning in terms of its capacity for being true or false.

This raises, however, a third question, which is closely connected with the two preceding: if it is impossible to step outside language in order to say how language agrees with reality and what it is that makes a proposition true, why does Wittgenstein still speak about 'representing', 'projecting', 'agreeing with reality', and so on? The answer is that beside all that can be said Wittgenstein leaves room for what cannot be said but can indeed be shown, or, more precisely, for what shows itself. Thus the agreement of a statement with reality is not logically demonstrable; it is seen, it manifests itself. 'A proposition *shows* its sense. A proposition *shows* how things stand *if* it is true' (4·022).

This view is akin to the doctrine of 'ostensive definitions' which was held by a number of logical positivists. The word 'ostensive', which is more or less synonymous with another word derived from Latin, 'demonstrative', and with the Greek word 'deictic', means 'pointing, showing'. A definition describes a certain concept by means of other concepts, which may in turn be defined by further concepts. But this cannot go on for ever. There comes a point, say the protagonists of ostensive definition, when one can give no more explanations, and one must then be content with pointing to what one means. If a visitor to Cambridge shrugs his shoulders when someone talks about 'King's College', because he has no idea of what the term means, then one can point to King's College and say, '*That is "King's College".*'

Wittgenstein does not himself defend ostensive definition. He does refer to it in a later work, but as a definition which has meaning only in connection with other data. Indeed, it would be difficult to call it 'definition' in the strict sense at all, because the point of it is precisely that one does not say anything, but lets something show itself by pointing it out. And this is how Wittgenstein argues; there is 'saying' and there is 'showing'. 'What can be shown, cannot be said' (4·1212).

All this is characteristic of Wittgenstein's logical atomism. There are in reality elementary constellations: states of affairs ('atomic facts' as they are called in the first translation, and with Wittgenstein's approval). These are projected in language in the form of simple propositions, such as '*p*' and '*q*'. This is already apparent at the beginning of the *Tractatus*, in the passage quoted. It is said here also that atomic facts are atomic in the particular sense that any one of them cannot be the case while everything else remains the same—it may not in fact be raining, but it is still cold, windy, slippery and so forth. The word 'atomic' expresses the contingent, accidental character of the world. Every state of affairs can be the case and also not be the case.

Connected with this is Wittgenstein's treatment of natural laws, which in many respects follows that of David Hume. 'The world divides into facts', as he writes at the beginning of his work (1·2). From this it follows that from one state of affairs one cannot infer another state of affairs. Every deduction occurs *a priori*; it is of a logical order and relates to logical rules, not to real situations (see 5·133–5·136; 6·36–6·361). 'It is an hypothesis that the sun will rise tomorrow: and this means that we do not *know* whether it will rise' (6·36311). Wittgenstein means by this that, while there may well be psychologically grounded expectations, there can only be talk of 'necessity' when this is of

51

a logical nature. So the law of causality, conceived as an explanation of natural events, is nothing but superstition (6·371; 6·372). It follows from this that the so-called law of causality is not something given in nature, but a certain logical form under which the statements of science can be ranged (cf. 6·32–6·34). Such 'laws' possess no physical 'must', but a logical 'must'; they do not belong to reality, but to language and the logical network. This critique of traditional ideas of causality is a direct consequence of his notion of the atomic isolation of the elements of reality, of states of affairs. Stegmüller has called this the 'mosaic theory' of language, as opposed to Wittgenstein's later conception, which he calls the 'chess theory'. Wittgenstein was also to take a closer look at the nature of nonphysical, logical necessity, as we shall see later on.

We should note here that behind or under the atomic facts there is something less contingent, what Wittgenstein calls the 'substance' of the world. His use of this idea reminds us in various ways of the philosophy of Leibniz. 'Substance is what subsists independently of what is the case' (2·024). And it is constituted, he maintains, by 'objects' (*Gegenstände*). By this we are not to understand ordinary physical objects, for these are contingent—they could have been other than they are, e.g., blue rather than red, large rather than small, etc. We have here a more logical concept. Leibniz had called the ultimate substances 'monads'. These were the realization of a logical world-structure, and each monad stood in relation to every other monad such that each mirrored the whole universe. These relations were not, as one might think, external and physical; they were contained within the isolated monad. Therefore they had a logical rather than physical character.

Leibniz often compared substance with the subject of a judgment—which was to accentuate even more the logical nature he ascribed to it. By 'subject' is meant in this case what is being spoken about in a judgment or proposition. In the judgment 'the table is round' the table is the subject and 'round' is the predicate. In classical logic a judgment like this is expressed as '*S* is *P*.' The relations between subject and predicate had been laid down already by Aristotle. For the term 'subject' he used a term which can be translated by the latin word 'substance'. He says of this logical substance that it cannot be predicated, that is to say, cannot fully be made into a predicate. Every judgment characterizes something by means of a predicate (red, round, etc.), but beneath there still remains the logical substance which is not a predicate.

Wittgenstein sees 'substance' as that which is not itself a predicate, but which possesses within itself every possible logical relation and which is made evident in propositions (e.g. 'the speck is black', 'the speck is red', 'the table is round'). Commentators such as Russell, Pitcher, Anscombe, Stenius, Griffin and Black are all concerned with the questions of what these substances ('objects' or 'things' as Wittgenstein variously calls them) could be, which are on the one hand 'empty', and on the other hand 'filled' by all the logical possibilities. They are all agreed on this, that they have nothing to do with actual, given objects, but are something like a logical substratum that can be recognized in every object. They differ as to where this substratum is to be found: in particular or in general concepts, or possibly even in properties. The disagreement is understandable, for it is by no means easy to expound a notion of 'objects' such as Wittgenstein's, when all that can be said of these objects is that they occur as components of a proposition and that, isolated from the state of affairs in which they occur (the roundness of the table, e.g.), they have no content whatever.

This becomes a little more comprehensible if we remember that for Wittgenstein the world is not built of elements or things (such as tables and raindrops), but of facts, of the occurrence and non-occurrence of states of affairs. Thus the opening passage of the *Tractatus* also becomes clearer: a state of affairs, as the primary datum, is already a combination of objects, which therefore cannot occur by themselves. 'It is essential to things that they should be possible constituents of states of affairs' (2·011). That is to say the speck *must* be either red or black or green, etc.—that is essential, necessary for the 'object'—but at the same time it is not necessary that the speck should be red, if such proves to be the case—a proposition to this effect would be contingent (2·0131). So an object must occur, if it occurs at all, in a certain coloured state of affairs, though in itself it is, so to speak, colourless (2·0232). 'Substance is what subsists independently of what is the case' (2·024). This statement, quoted once already, now becomes clearer. Whatever is the case is accidental and contingent, and in virtue of this a proposition can turn out to be true or false. But the substance which is projected in the proposition as a logical substratum is necessary, for it is present in *every* possible relation in which it can occur (being red, on the table, on the ground, etc.). This talk of substance is concerned with logical form, with what can be said of an 'object' in logical terms, apart from the factual state of affairs. It is concerned, so to speak, with the *how* of an object, rather than the *that* (cf. the statements quoted at the beginning, 2·012, 2·014, 2·0141). This is evident also from a statement like the following: 'If I know an object I also know all its possible occurrences in states of affairs. (Every one of these possibilities must be part of the nature of the object.) A new possibility cannot be discovered later' (2·0123). Here is *a priori* talk of the object, which is not based on uncertain experience (*a posteriori*). In a proposition objects or things are represented by names ('speck', 'glass', etc.); and one can *only* name them, and not also pass judgment on them ('put them into words'); one can only say *how* a thing is, not *what* it is (3·221).

We can say in summing up that objects occur only in configurations of states of affairs and, as a corollary, that names occur only in the combination of a judgment ('*p*'). It would be possible, logically, to indicate all the possible configurations, and thus to map out, as it were, the whole of logical space. In fact only one configuration occurs. 'Objects are what is unalterable and subsistent; their configuration is what is changing and unstable' (2·0271). The *possibility* of such a configuration is the logical form, which can be investigated irrespective of the factual occurrence of a concrete state of affairs. So the logical form determines both propositions and 'objects', in so far as these are as yet 'unfilled' by a factual situation—not as yet red or blue, for example. The logical form is what is held in common by reality and the pictures or structures of language which represent this reality (see e.g. 2·18). We have come full circle to the point with which we started: Wittgenstein's doctrine of the projection of reality in logically formed language.

Bertrand Russell has called the *Tractatus* the first philosophy of logic. It should at least be clear from the foregoing exposition that Wittgenstein's discussion of the function and possibilities of logic deal at the same time with philosophical problems of the past. The world consists of states of affairs, not of things. These constellations can be reproduced in a picture, rather as the course of events in a car accident, for example, might be retraced in a court of law by the use of models (see *Notebooks*). It is a case of projection in a picture, says Wittgenstein, and he has in mind the kind of method advocated by Marcus Hertz in mechanics. It is not so much a case of reflection, therefore, because Wittgenstein also compares the picture and the reality with the score and the music. Everyday language reproduces actual situations, but these are extremely complicated and often opaque when seen through an impure use of words. Logical analysis brings clarification and the logical statement or proposition, therefore, functions particularly well as a picture of reality.

These propositions, as we have also seen, derive their meaning from the possibility of their being true or false. This shows itself; it cannot be said. Within the field of language itself—logical space—one can only point out the possibilities of a situation actually occurring. Similarly, the object is a factually incomplete element, in so far as it never occurs unqualified, detached from a course of events, while on the other hand it is characterized logically by all the possible states of affairs in which it *can* occur.

So that which shows itself, the factual occurrence of a situation, is a specification, as it were, of what is given in the logical network as a possibility. Logical language forms a network because all operations are closely interwoven. One operation (as indicated by a constant '&' or 'v') can be reduced to another. Ultimately, this happens according to sequences which carry no truth-conditions (i.e. as to whether they are applicable or non-applicable to a concrete situation) and which are therefore always true because they are tautological (e.g. $p \lor \sim p$). Thus logical constants do not allow for new factual possibilities, but as substitute symbols they mark out together the whole of logical space. Propositions (such as p, q, r, etc.) do of course indicate various possibilities. Each of itself is contingent in the sense that it may or may not be the case. Taken together the possibilities increase: for one proposition there are two possibilities, for two propositions four, for three propositions eight. These possibilities are to be inferred from the 'picture', and so in this case from language (propositions)—we can see *how* a situation would be *if* it were to arise. But *that* it arises is not to be inferred from the logical network.

Here again we find Wittgenstein agreeing with Leibniz, who saw the factual existing world as one of a number of possible worlds. Logical truths (*vérités de raison*) can, according to Leibniz, be expressed in advance (*a priori*) and concern the logical world-possibilities; factual truths (*vérités de fait*) can be established only after the event (*a posteriori*) and concern this contingent, factually given world. Wittgenstein draws the line between logical space and factual world even more sharply— Leibniz had still tried, by way of a certain metaphysical principle, to derive the factual world from the logical world. Wittgenstein sponsors on the one hand an atomistic interpretation: independent propositions (any one can be dropped and the rest remain the same) which represent states of affairs. At the same time, as Black for example has emphasized, there is clearly a more organic conception: the coherence of propositions, the possibilities according to which elements in a situation can appear, forms one connected network.

But in what way then does this logical network correspond to specific, contingent reality? The network can have very different forms. Many logical systems are possible and they can function as structures of various sciences (in mathematics, for example, but also in mechanics). A net as such, therefore, says nothing as yet about the factual world—one may recall what was said earlier about Wittgenstein's view of causality as a logical relation. Though it does tell us this about the world, that we can work better with the one network than we can with the other (cf. *Notebooks*, pp. 35 seq; *Tract.*, 6·34 seq). An image which Wittgenstein often uses is that of a measure. The measure 'does not say that an object to be measured is a yard long'. For the division of the scale (the *how*, the logical relations, etc.) is there beforehand. It is only afterwards that we learn whether a particular measure is applicable or not (cf. 2·1511; 4·0312; 6·32; *Notebooks*, pp. 37, 38, 41). But must not the measure be accommodated to the field of investigation? This question becomes prominent in Wittgenstein's later work and the analysis of this possibility leads him to speak of a variety of measures!

Thus Wittgenstein develops a logic of speech. What can be

said can be said clearly. If misunderstandings or dilemmas arise, this is because we have failed to give precise meaning to the symbols of our language. Now, in order properly to see the linguistic sign as a symbol we must observe its meaningful use, and this use follows certain logical rules, the 'logical grammar' or 'logical syntax' as Wittgenstein calls them (3·323–3·327). The logical operations are mutually connected, form one network, so that with one operation all the others are given as well. The limits of what can be said, therefore, are defined by the logical rules. 'The limits of my language mean the limits of my world' (5·6). For the logic of language shows *how* elements fit states of affairs and how states of affairs in wider constellations can be linked together. Not that we can decide on the basis of this logic what situation is actually to be found in the world, but only what can be found—thus not the *that* but the *how*. In other words, 'I can only deny that the picture fits, but I cannot deny the picture' (*Notebooks*, p. 33). The logic of speech provides a compelling analysis of human speech and thought, but it shows at the same time that there are a number of questions, namely those connected with factual existence, which cannot be answered by logic. But 'if logic can be completed without answering certain questions, then it *must* be completed *without* answering them' (*Notebooks*, p. 3).

CHAPTER THREE

The Metaphysics of Silence

'4·113 Philosophy sets limits to the much disputed sphere of natural science.

4·114 It must set limits to what can be thought; and, in doing so, to what cannot be thought. It must set limits to what cannot be thought by working outwards through what can be thought.

4·115 It will signify what cannot be said, by presenting clearly what can be said.

4·116 Everything that can be thought at all can be thought clearly. Everything that can be put into words can be put clearly.

4·12 Propositions can represent the whole of reality, but they cannot represent what they must have in common with reality in order to be able to represent it—logical form. In order to be able to represent logical form, we should have to be able to station ourselves with propositions somewhere outside logic, that is to say outside the world.

4·121 Propositions cannot represent logical form: it is mirrored in them. What finds its reflection in language, language cannot represent. What expresses *itself* in language, *we* cannot express by means of language. Propositions *show* the logical form of reality. They display it.'

THESE propositions from the *Tractatus* argue once again that a statement has meaning in so far as it reproduces a state of affairs. Yet it 'reproduces' it by way of experiment (*probeweise*, cf. 4·031) or by way of a model, for what the statement has in common with the state of affairs is the logical form, the possibility of a state of affairs occurring or not occurring. That a situation does *in fact* occur cannot be expressed in language, any more than the fact that the logical form of language agrees with the form of reality. One can only point to the form of reality. Indeed, the proposition itself brings it into view, it 'displays' it.

Wittgenstein makes no distinction between language and thought. From the logical point of view, this is quite understandable, for factual psychological problems are irrelevant here. If something is said to be 'thinkable', this is only to say that we can picture it to ourselves; we cannot think of anything illogically (3–3·032). But we can surely think of the most absurd and fantastic situations? We can surely imagine things for which we could find no words? Certainly, but not in such a way that they would in the strict sense be illogical. We could not imagine a speck, for example, that was entirely and at the same time pure red and pure black; nor that it was both raining and not raining at the same time and place. (If we then say that we can well think of such a state of affairs by imagining the kind of mist of which we cannot say that it either does or does not contain rain, we are still thinking logically. Is it now raining, or isn't it? '$p \lor \sim p$', but never '$p \ \& \sim p$'.)

This means not only that we cannot, strictly, think illogical thoughts, but also that we cannot express them. We can of course talk meaningless language, as it often happens that we do, but then we have failed to understand which logical or 'syntactical' role the words are meant to play. Essentially, we are still thinking logically, and the *Tractatus* offers a series of recommendations on how to avoid senseless language and to be clear about the logic of the language we normally use.

It follows from this that so long as one obeys the logical rules it is impossible to talk nonsense, or even to ask an illogical question. If one does in fact ask such a question, someone can always point out an improper use of words or an illogical relation between meanings of words, so that the question can then be reformulated in a purely logical way. But this also means that one cannot put a question to which no answer could be given. Wittgenstein says therefore that when an answer cannot be put into words, neither can the question be put into words; and that the riddle does not exist (6·5). Scepticism, he continues, is not irrefutable, but nonsensical, because it raises doubts, and must raise them, where no question can be answered, and thus where, logically speaking, no question can be asked. He therefore differs radically from the sceptic Mauthner, though he learned much from Mauthner's critique of language. In his own critique of language, Wittgenstein used logical analysis to show precisely the meaninglessness of apparent profundities (riddles) and of negative doubt (4·0031).

Yet this logical conception of language depends on the view that the logical form of reality is mirrored in language, a view which cannot itself be affirmed in a judgment. So the rejection of the riddle as meaningless is only possible by virtue of what cannot be said or thought, but yet shows itself. This tension, so characteristic of Wittgenstein's thought, is epitomized in the words with which in 1918 he concluded the preface to the *Tractatus*: 'On the other hand the *truth* of the thoughts that are here set forth seems to me unassailable and definitive. I therefore believe myself to have found, on all essential points, the final solution of the problems. And if I am not mistaken in this belief, then the second thing in which the value of this work consists is that it shows how little is achieved when these problems are solved.'

This appraisal of his own work tells us something of Wittgen-

stein's intentions: to dissolve the vexatious questions of metaphysics by the clear force of logical analysis. Yet these 'questions', which cannot be formulated or even thought, still need
to be reckoned with. On the one hand, these are questions which
Wittgenstein had already raised: the logical structure of language is a measure that we construct ourselves—about that
which we ourselves construct we can say something in advance—
about a state of affairs we can only speak after the event, though
the agreement between reality and logical form, which reality
has in common with language, can only be 'shown'. The big
question, however, is what this logical measure is to be used for
(cf. 6·211). A further question, which occurred already in the
last chapter, is whether the measure should be applied to the
field of investigation—a question that is to play an important
role in Wittgenstein's later thought.

Behind these, however, lie other, metaphysical questions.
There are many possible constellations, world-configurations;
but why is it that *this* world, of all worlds, actually exists? It is
the question of the facticity, or the contingency of the world. It
had been formulated as such by Leibniz and Schopenhauer,
but for Wittgenstein it is unsayable and unthinkable, and
therefore meaningless, though, as we shall see, it still presents
itself in Wittgenstein's work. In some notes on logic (from 1913)
Wittgenstein writes that philosophy does not provide pictures
of reality and does not undertake a scientific investigation of the
facts: it consists rather of logic and metaphysics, the first being
the basis for the second. In his *Tractatus* the metaphysical
question occupies much of his attention, and 'he manages to say
a good deal about what cannot be said' (Bertrand Russell,
Introduction to the *Tractatus*, p. xxi).

Thus Wittgenstein writes in his *Notebook* of 1916: 'What do
I know about God and the purpose of life? I know that this
world exists. That I am placed in it like my eye in its visual field.

That something about it is problematic, which we call its meaning. That this meaning does not lie in it but outside it. That life is the world. That my will penetrates the world. That my will is good or evil. Therefore that good and evil are somehow connected with the meaning of the world. The meaning of life, i.e. the meaning of the world, we can call God. And connect with this the comparison of God to a father. To pray is to think about the meaning of life. I cannot bend the happenings of the world to my will: I am completely powerless. . . . If good or evil willing affects the world it can only affect the boundaries of the world, not the facts, what cannot be portrayed by language but can only be shown in language' (pp. 72, 73).

These notes, followed by others in similar vein, are the deposit of that 'thinking aloud' which is so characteristic of Wittgenstein's style. They are developed further in the still more condensed statements of the *Tractatus* about what can be shown but cannot be said. The 'showing' is related to the will and to the attitude of the will with regard to the meaning of life. The influence of some of Schopenhauer's ideas is unmistakable here. 'It would be possible to say (*à la* Schopenhauer): It is not the world of Idea that is either good or evil, but the willing subject' (*Notebooks*, p. 79).

That there is also a difference between Wittgenstein and Schopenhauer is equally clear, since for Schopenhauer the world of Idea is such that its form can be fully clarified by logical analysis and fully expressed in logical language, as conceived already by Leibniz. Moreover, Schopenhauer's metaphysics, as that of the dark motive force of the will, can do nothing to explain the world of concepts. (This Mauthner also had argued.) For while the will is important for Wittgenstein with respect to the meaning of life, it cannot be expressed in words.

But why should this be so? Because the will is not directed to what might possibly occur, but to what actually does occur, to which it may or may not give assent. The human will does not resign itself to facts. 'To believe in a God means to see that the facts of the world are not the end of the matter' (*Notebooks*, p. 74). But *that* something is the case is precisely what cannot be said in language, only that this or that thing could or could not be the case. Therefore the will can be directed only to what is shown but not said, to the whole form of the world.

It is worth noting that 'world' and 'life' in Wittgenstein are very closely linked. It was pointed out earlier that the 'world' refers not so much to the universe as to the whole space in which events occur. The limits of my language are the limits of my world (5·6). But also: 'the world and life are one' (5·621). 'Life is the world' (*Notebooks*, p. 77). Thus he raises the 'unanswerable' and therefore unsayable question of the meaning of life. It is true that in his later philosophy life can to some degree be expressed—its pattern can be traced in what Wittgenstein called 'language-games'. But in the *Tractatus* there is no question of language-games. There is only a mosaic (to use Stegmüller's phrase), lifeless fragments of language, atomic propositions. And these propositions, with the logical possibilities of their combination and transformation, mark out the space of what can be said.

Now, 'the world is all that is the case' (1). 'The world is independent of my will' (6·373). The moral will, therefore, can bring about nothing in the world, for the world contains only that which is logically connected and can be logically formulated, that is to say, which can be said and thought. So ethical propositions are also impossible. If the will changes something, it is not a fact within the world but the world itself, in so far as this world is identical with life, or in so far as it is 'my world'. 'If the good or bad exercise of the will does alter the world, it can alter only the limits of the world, not the facts—not what can be expressed by means of language. In short the effect must be that it becomes an altogether different world. It must, so to speak, wax and wane as a whole. The world of the happy man is a different one from that of the unhappy man' (6·43).

What was said earlier in connection with the *Notebooks* now acquires a new perspective; the world of facts, the world of meaningful language—where language may correspond with states of affairs and assumes a logical structure—allows no room for the will, moral values or questions of happiness and the meaning of life. This is what Schopenhauer called the world as Idea. The world that is my world, however, the world as identical with life, the world as a total form, which can wax and wane—this does involve ethics and the human will to alter the world. This is what Schopenhauer called the world as Will. Where Wittgenstein differs from Schopenhauer, and differs widely, is in his complete rejection of metaphysics in the ordinary sense, that is, as a philosophical system. The world as Will can*not* be expressed in words, but shows itself, though in saying this all has been said. In one respect Wittgenstein stands closer to Kant, who also rejected metaphysics as a system, setting logical limits to knowledge and speaking of metaphysical ideas as 'frontier guards', which point to their practical function in ethics. (This he developed in his *Critique of Practical Reason*.) It is true that in Kant's transcendental idealism the limits of experience are narrower than the limits of what can be said (ethics can still be expressed), whereas in Wittgenstein's 'transcendental lingualism' (Stenius' phrase) the two limits coincide. In this respect Wittgenstein stands between Hume, for whom the limitation of knowledge has a purely sceptical value, no ethical value, and Kant, for whom the limitation of knowledge creates a positive opening for ethics.

The world as Will, about which ultimately one can only be silent, has a correlate in what is even less expressible in words:

the 'I' or the subject. Thus Wittgenstein writes in his *Notebooks*, 'Good and evil only enter through the *subject*. And the subject is not part of the world, but a boundary of the world' (p. 79). In the *Tractatus* he says of the subject that it is never found as an object in the world, though the world is nevertheless the world as I find it, which is to say it is my world. Similarly, what I see is my visual field, but the eye which sees it all cannot itself be seen, as an object in the visual field. The subject, which he refers to here as the 'metaphysical subject', is a limit of the world (5·63–5·641).

If we look over again the statements cited in this chapter, two things should become apparent. First, that Wittgenstein is really advocating an extreme version of positivism. We should fail to do him justice if, in reaction against a too narrowly positivist interpretation, we should make him out to be a kind of mystic or metaphysician. He does touch on a number of metaphysical themes—more examples will be given in what follows—but he also rejects metaphysics in the sense that he considers it impossible to build a system, or even to say anything meaningful systematically about these very questions with which he is also concerned. The task of philosophy, as appears in the quotation at the beginning of this chapter, is to set limits to what can be thought, to present clearly what can be said. By doing this Wittgenstein has solved definitively, to his own satisfaction, the main problems of philosophy.

On the other hand, in taking his positivist viewpoint to the limits, he clearly recognizes the limitation on what can be positively said and thought. It is here then that we meet the other side of Wittgenstein's thought which we may call the metaphysical or the mystical—provided we understand by this, not that he intends to supplement his positivism with something else, a metaphysical doctrine, but that within it he wishes to define as clearly as possible the positive capacity of thought and speech. He may then make the far from dogmatic or positivist statement that little has been achieved when these problems are solved! He can also point to what is the reverse side of logical speech, namely, 'showing'. Determining what can be thought is now a matter of setting limits to what *cannot* be thought by working outwards through what can be thought; it is a matter of clearly presenting what can be said as a way of indicating what cannot be said (4·113; 4·114).

Logic, wrote Wittgenstein in 1913, must precede metaphysics. It became clear in the *Tractatus* that it allowed only a few, short statements which themselves are meaningless and only point to what cannot be said. The term 'metaphysics' does not occur again in the *Tractatus* except as an adjective, 'metaphysical subject', and once in the sense of a metaphysical statement; which is then rejected. But there is another term which replaces the term 'metaphysics' in order to emphasize that 'metaphysics' is not to be expressed in words and is only to be shown: the term 'the mystical'. This is not to say 'mysticism', for this again can be a doctrine, a connected body of statements, the very possibility of which—at least in the form of meaningful language —Wittgenstein denies. The mystical points rather to what manifests itself, and precisely when there is nothing to be said.

'6·432 *How* things are in the world is a matter of complete indifference for what is higher. God does not reveal himself *in* the world. 6·4321 The facts all contribute only to setting the problem, not to its solution. 6·44 It is not *how* things are in the world that is mystical, but *that* it exists. 6·45 To view the world *sub specie aeterni* is to view it as a whole—a limited whole. Feeling the world as a limited whole is the mystical.' That this world now exists, as a stubborn fact which the will, in its quest for happiness and the meaning of life, can rebel against, is something derived from logical analysis. For it concerns the question of 'how', as we explained in the previous chapter. To see the world as a whole, and as such a limited world, is to reach beyond its limitedness, to raise questions outside the world of facts, like the question of God's existence. In this context Wittgenstein employs an expression derived from Spinoza, just as the title of his book also recalls the work of this Dutch philosopher. Spinoza, on various occasions, used the phrase '*sub specie aeternitatis*', in the light of eternity. This refers to the highest form of knowledge, which is no longer purely mathematical or logical, but can transcend the relations of time ('*absque ulla temporis relatione*'), that is, can see things from God's point of view (cf. *Ethics* II, prop. 44).

Wittgenstein believes that, whereas one cannot alter the course of things in the universe, one can change one's view of it. This idea is also to be found in Spinoza, and, in some respects, goes back to the Stoic view of life. But Wittgenstein draws out a further implication : if one considers just how the questions of life make themselves manifest outside the sphere of time and of logical relations it becomes clear that there is nothing more to be said about them. The mystical is a 'solution', but not in the ordinary sense of a solution to a riddle, for this can only be given in terms of the logical space of meaningful language. 'The solution of the riddle of life in space and time lies *outside* space and time' (6·4312). So again, it is not a solution in the ordinary sense, for, as Wittgenstein says, when all meaningful, scientific questions have been answered, the problems of life remain completely untouched; of course there are then no questions left, and this itself is the answer (6·52). Does Wittgenstein mean all this to be negative, in that the mystical is to be understood as a bewitchment by meaningless language and therefore in essence non-existent? No, for while it cannot be made intelligible as a problem, it is there nonetheless; 'The inexpressible does indeed exist. It *shows* itself, it is the mystical' (6·522). Where Wittgenstein differs from metaphysicians like Spinoza and Schopenhauer, and even from a critical thinker like Kant, is in assimilating what cannot be said to what cannot be thought. Thinking is not a separate activity, outside or alongside the operations with symbols in language. The mystical, therefore, is not something that could be thought about apart from language. It is not something in addition to other things, but merely the limitedness of thought and language as setting bounds to what cannot be thought. And as such it becomes apparent in clear thinking and meaningful language.

The question of the meaning of life is not a genuine question, because there is no answer to give to it. By 'question' and 'answer' Wittgenstein means that which can be said, which can be uttered in meaningful propositions. 'Meaningful' here has a different connotation to what he calls 'the meaning of life'. A proposition has meaning if one can tell from it in what circumstances it would be true and in what circumstances false, if, that is, one can hold it as a kind of measure against the factual states of affairs. In this way all propositions are of equal value. However, as soon as one reflects on the will, and thus on the strictly inadmissible and inexpressible 'question' of the meaning of life, one is no longer dealing with the 'equal value' of all propositions and of possible states of affairs. One is now vexed with the question of there being a world at all, and one is therefore concerned with a meaning *attributed* to the world by the will. It is a question not of facts but of values.

From his discussion of these problems of values and the meaning of the world Wittgenstein draws conclusions which are already implicit in his view of the mystical. A value, which makes the factual, contingent existence of the world in a profounder sense necessary and acceptable, can never be found in the world. Spinoza believed that he had obtained a knowledge in the light of eternity by which, as he said, the contingent could be seen from God's point of view to be necessary. Leibniz tried to bridge the gulf between the basic operations of a necessary logic and the basic tendencies of this factual and contingent world. Schopenhauer went so far as to base logical rules on the irrational fact of the dark human will. Wittgenstein sees in this whole sphere of problems good reason to limit himself to what can be said logically, clearly and intersubjectively. Whatever makes the world non-contingent, he says, can no longer itself be *in* the world and within the bounds of language and thought. In the world everything is as it is and happens as it happens, so that no value is to be discovered here. Everything which concerns itself with values, such as ethics and aesthetics, proves in the event to be an impossible undertaking. Ethics and aesthetics, he writes, cannot be formulated in definitive judgments. Even such a doctrine as the immortality of the soul, so fundamental for Kant and Schopenhauer, can provide no 'solution', for meaning and value lie always outside the world of facts and of language (cf. 6·41–6·421; 6·431–6.4312).

Spinoza made a distinction between intellectual knowledge, acquired through logic and within the limits of the temporal world, and rational, mystical 'intuition', which leads to knowledge in the light of eternity. One meets the distinction later as one between knowledge of the understanding and knowledge of reason. For Kant, reason (*Vernunft*) is the highest organ of knowledge, and while it does not yield a substantial metaphysics, it does provide a functional metaphysics; that is to say, it transcends the scientific knowledge of the understanding in the discovery of the limits of this knowledge. The certain knowledge of the sciences implies this limitedness, while beyond it one may, by means of 'practical reason', command a view of the moral life of man. In contemporary philosophy some features of Kantian thinking are to be found in Karl Jaspers. He employs Kantian terminology and subscribes to a kind of regulative metaphysics, as a doctrine of the bounds of human knowledge.

THE METAPHYSICS OF SILENCE

The mystical, as something inexpressible—Jaspers calls it Transcendence—cannot be spoken of in ordinary language, but only in so far as it manifests itself in the concealed, indirect manner that Jaspers calls the 'cipher'.

Wittgenstein has much in common with this Kantian view. To formulate as lucidly and logically as possible what can be said is at the same time to signify what cannot be said. To show as exactly as possible what are the structures of language is, on the one hand, to dispel the misunderstandings and pseudo-problems of metaphysics as a system, but, on the other hand, to establish that in some indirect way the metaphysical or the mystical does properly manifest itself. His whole philosophy of logic, as Russell called Wittgenstein's *Tractatus*, becomes itself a kind of 'cipher', because it frequently comes up against something that really cannot be said, but which nevertheless shows itself. It is true that what shows itself varies according to the subject under discussion: the form of the picture which the picture displays (2·172), the name as a sign of a thing, where the application of the sign shows what is not said in the sign itself (3·262), the proposition shows its meaning, that is to say, how things stand if something is the case (4·022), the proposition shows the logical form of reality (4·121), the limits of language show that the world is my world (5·62), the mystical manifests itself (6·522). But one common theme may be seen in all this, namely, the connection between language and reality, the applicability of logical measures to contingent states of affairs, the insertion of a factual world (the 'that') in the broad logical network of possible occurrences (the 'how'), and above all how the limitedness of each network of language is apparent in all this, since none can accommodate the will or give expression to values. So Wittgenstein raises classical, metaphysical questions, though he does this with negative effect, in so far as the questions, once raised, evaporate as meaningless.

71

THE METAPHYSICS OF SILENCE

This last point indicates the difference between Wittgenstein's statements on the mystical which shows itself and, for example, Jaspers' doctrine of the cipher at the boundary of language and life. Jaspers presents a philosophy in which indeed much can be said in terms of the personal awareness of cipherlanguage. For Wittgenstein the argument breaks off just there, for there is nothing further to be said. In this respect Wittgenstein is even more radical than Kant. For while Kant also cried down metaphysical talk in the philosophy of his time, he made room for language expressing man's awareness of moral duty, in which the concepts 'God', 'freedom' and 'immortality'—which are dealt with by Wittgenstein also—are formulated in the indirect language of 'requirements' or 'postulates', a language exceeding the limits of what can be analysed logically. Wittgenstein was more radical in the sense that he considered even such formulations impossible and placed the constitutive operations of the will, the consciousness of moral and practical life, wholly outside the scope of philosophy and in the world of common activities. For this reason he gave up philosophy and became a gardener and a village school teacher.

This practical and positivist attitude is the final outcome of Wittgenstein's *Tractatus*. Certainly, there is a fragment of metaphysics in his philosophy—in his picture theory of language, his logical atomism, the doctrine of the mystical. But then his metaphysics, as expressed in his analysis of language, is a metaphysics of silence. Philosophy is an activity, not a system; it is a clarification of language with a view to saying only what can be said. It is not one science among others, and most certainly not a super-science—in this sense it is *not* metaphysics. To do metaphysics and 'show' what cannot be said in the spirit of Wittgenstein one needs first to be a good positivist: to give a logical elucidation of language, and to demonstrate to anyone who propounds a metaphysical system that he is talking a meaningless language, making statements from which it is not at all clear how they could ever be true or false. The correct language is that of logic, mathematics, etc. (consisting of tautologies), plus those statements which can be verified, namely, all that is embraced by the natural sciences.

Two questions arise here. Is there anything left that we may call the proper sphere of philosophy? The answer could only be 'no'. But then has not Wittgenstein himself said far too much when he used words like 'will', 'the meaning of life', 'God', 'the mystical'? Indeed he has, and he also says that one understands this properly only if one perceives that it was not really possible to express all this in language. Mauther's comparison of language with a ladder one must throw away is used by Wittgenstein in another connection by comparing his own statements *about* language—about what can and what cannot be said—with a ladder one climbs, but which one must then throw away. His work ends with a thesis of only one sentence, indicating the necessary role of silence.

This can be said most clearly, however, in the compact theses that close the *Tractatus*:

'6·53 The correct method in philosophy would really be the following: to say nothing except what can be said, i.e. propositions of natural science—i.e. something that has nothing to do with philosophy—and then, whenever someone else wanted to say something metaphysical, to demonstrate to him that he had failed to give a meaning to certain signs in his propositions. Although it would not be satisfying to the other person—he would not have the feeling that we were teaching him philosophy—*this* method would be the only strictly correct one.

6·54 My propositions serve as elucidations in the following way: anyone who understands me eventually recognizes them as nonsensical, when he has used them—as steps—to climb up beyond them. (He must, so to speak, throw away the ladder after he has climbed up it.)

7   What we cannot speak about we must pass over in silence.'

CHAPTER FOUR

Language-Games

'The more narrowly we examine actual language, the sharper becomes the conflict between it and our require- ment. (For the crystalline purity of logic was, of course, not a *result of investigation*: it was a requirement.) The conflict becomes intolerable; the requirement is now in danger of becoming empty.—We have got on to slippery ice where there is no friction and so in a certain sense the conditions are ideal, but also, just because of that, we are unable to walk. We want to walk: so we need *friction*. Back to the rough ground!'

Philosophical Investigations, p. 46, § 107

'. . . Ask yourself whether our language is complete— whether it was so before the symbolism of chemistry and the notation of the infinitesimal calculus were incorporated in it; for these are, so to speak, suburbs of our language. (And how many houses or streets does it take before a town begins to be a town?) Our language can be seen as an ancient city: a maze of little streets and squares, of old and new houses, and of houses with additions from various periods; and this surrounded by a multitude of new boroughs with straight regular streets and uniform houses.'

Ibid, p. 8, §18

WHEN Wittgenstein returned to Cambridge in 1929, a number of ideas had ripened in his mind, particularly his ideas on language. Since he always saw a close connection between

75

language and thought, and between philosophy and the rules that govern the uses of a language, his ideas were of direct philosophical significance. The most important of these was that he no longer conceived language as uniform, and further, that he had no desire now to model factual language on the language of logic. Originally, in the *Tractatus*, Wittgenstein wanted to follow Russell in setting up a kind of logical calculus, which could bring to light the *one* hidden structure of every factual language. This proved to be impossible, however, and he was now more strongly influenced by Moore, in so far as he turned his attention to the language of actual use. Logical language, with its laws (tautologies), provided no points of friction with everyday reality. Therefore Wittgenstein turned back to the rough ground, came to wander in the labyrinth of old, historic streets, marked by the passage of time, instead of taking the straight lanes of fixed notations in artificial languages.

This programme, set out in the main work of his final period, had been developed some time before. He wrote a book in 1929, *Philosophische Bemerkungen*, that was published only recently, in 1964. This work, together with a later, as yet unpublished manuscript and some dictated notes from the years 1933–35 (*The Blue and Brown Books*), form the transition to his final period. But already in 1929 he seems to have adopted his broader outlook on language. True, it is still logic that must investigate language, even ordinary language (*Ph.B.*, p. 52, §3), but he points out also that there are innumerable ways in which language is used, and which certainly cannot be read off the surface of language on the basis of ordinary grammar. Verbs, nouns, etc., can each be used in very different ways. To imagine, for example, that a noun indicates something which exists (such as 'thought') gives rise to serious misunderstandings. 'The nature of language, however, is a picture of the nature of the world; and philosophy as a guardian of grammar can actually grasp the nature of the world, only not in the propositions of language, but in the rules for this language, which exclude meaningless combinations of signs.' (*Ph.B.*, p. 85, §54.)

Much of this is reminiscent of the *Tractatus*. Yet it makes all the clearer the distinction between 'surface grammar', that is, grammar as it appears on the surface, and 'depth grammar', that is, the probing analysis of the innumerable, sometimes incomplete forms of language as these are to be discovered in factual language. (These terms also occur in the *Philosophical Investigations*.) When the depth grammar is discovered, it appears to involve some very simple rules, though these are extremely difficult to apply in the tangle of uses that we maintain in everyday language. This provides an answer to the question as to why philosophy is so complicated, says Wittgenstein, for it disentangles the knots that we have meaninglessly tied in our own thinking, and must therefore go through just such complicated motions as brought about these tangles (*Ph.B.*, p. 153, §133; p. 52, §2).

This theme recurs throughout Wittgenstein's work. Language is as complicated as a living organism—so he wrote in the *Tractatus*—but for this reason we must discover the *life* in this organism, if, that is, we are looking for clarity and simplicity as the essence and meaning of the complexities of language—such is the concern of his later writings. This does not mean that he wants merely to return to everyday language, as some have supposed. He is not propounding a sober, commonsense philosophy, and in that respect he departs from many British philosophers, like Moore. 'There is no commonsense answer to a philosophical problem. One can defend common sense against the attacks of philosophers only by solving their puzzles, i.e., by curing them of the temptation to attack common sense; not by restating the views of common sense. A philosopher is not a man out of his senses, a man who doesn't see what everybody sees' (*The Blue and Brown Books*—abbreviated, *B.B.B.*—pp. 58, 59). Wittgenstein continues with an indication of his own programme: we find that there is puzzlement and indeed mental discomfort, not only when we fail to understand certain facts—this is where science must help—but also when the systems or notations of our language dissatisfy us—here philosophy must step in. Our ordinary language, which of all languages is the one which pervades all our life, holds our mind rigidly in *one* position, and this causes a mental cramp. The task of philosophy is to remove this mental cramp.

Philosophical elucidation, therefore, must effect a kind of depth-therapy. It must penetrate so far into the function of language and thought that puzzlement and mental cramp give way to insight into the simplicity of living language. In 1929 Wittgenstein, as we have said, used the image of untying a knot. In *The Blue and Brown Books* he talks about a jigsaw puzzle: it seems as though we had either the wrong pieces, or not enough of them, to put together our jigsaw puzzle; but they are all there, only all mixed up. We must therefore not try to force or distort them, but first look at them carefully and only then arrange them (*B.B.B.*, p. 46). In his last writings philosophy is seen as an analysis of different language-games, where a game of chess is often used as a model for the rules of the language. 'Philosophy is a battle against the bewitchment of our intelligence by means of language' (*Philosophical Investigations*—abbreviated, *Ph.I.*—p. 47, §109). Philosophy must let everything be seen just as it is—look carefully at the pieces of the puzzle and only then put them together. It criticizes language only when it is running idle (*Ph.I.*, pp. 49–51). Philosophy is: to help the fly out of the bottle into which it has flown. Philosophical dissatisfaction disappears by our seeing *more*. To resolve philosophical problems one compares things which it has never seriously occurred to anyone to compare. (See *Remarks on the Foundations of Mathematics*, pp. 109, 170.)

It was pointed out at the beginning of this chapter that Wittgenstein abandoned his previous position, that it was possible by means of logic to reveal the hidden structure of ordinary language. In his later period he argues that to persist in the view that there must be *one* definite meaning (that can be schematized logically) in a given piece of language is to invite mental cramp. There are in fact as many meanings in language as there are ways of employing it in everyday life. There are *many* language-games, each of which is justified within the human situation in which it applies.

In the *Philosophische Bemerkungen* we have a transition phase. It is still argued that language, even ordinary language, has an underlying logic, but there appears to be a greater variety in this logic than was recognized in the *Tractatus*. In the earlier book Wittgenstein had remarked that a speck in the visual field could be either red or blue, but not both simultaneously. This led to extensive argumentations, which proved to have far-reaching consequences. He argued that one can draw logical conclusions in virtue of the tautological structure of combined propositions. As 'p & q' is a contingent proposition (with the truth-values: *TFFF*—see Chapter Two), so '$\sim(p$ & $\sim p)$' is a necessary proposition, a logical law, which invariably yields the truth-value 'true' (or in the case of the contradiction, 'p & $\sim p$', invariably false). However, in 1929 he wrote that if it is established as a logical necessity that a speck cannot be both red and green at the same time, it would be possible to set down concerning a given element (f): '$f(g)$ & $f(r)$', in order to establish in the case of a speck not being both red and green that the two are contradictory (*Ph.B.*, pp. 105–14).

A number of marginal notes should be made here. First, it is obvious that '$f(g)$ & $f(r)$' has a different logical behaviour to '*p* & *q*', for in the latter case there are a number of truth-possibilities (viz., *TFFF*), while these are lacking in the first case. That is to say 'that the "&" here has a different meaning' (*Ph.B.*, p. 107, §79). Evidently, in the case of the mutually exclusive properties the logical notation of logic itself is being used differently—one could also say another logic was being used. Connected with this, undoubtedly, is the fact that the symbols employed, '*f(g)*' and '*f(r)*', imply the logical form of colour and space, and with this the impossibility of two colours occupying the same place at the same time. If the same symbol is used at one moment for a colour and at another for a sound, this would mean that it is not actually the same symbol at all, because it would be applied according to different rules, or, to put it technically, because different syntactical rules would be valid for that symbol.

This leads to a second point. In the example given the rules concern the truth-functions of an elementary part of a proposition. In the *Tractatus* these truth-functions were confined to complete propositions; now a new field is opened. This has at least two consequences. First, that necessary, logical propositions are not made up entirely of tautologies. Tautologies occur only in the form of combined propositions (such as '*p* v ~*p*', '~*q* v (~*p* v *q*)', etc.). Propositions that are not combined cannot as such lead to logical conclusions. This is connected with the logical atomism of the *Tractatus* period, where something can be the case or not be the case and everything else remains the same. Atomic statements stand apart from each other, so that one cannot conclude from one to the other. This conception Wittgenstein abandoned. He takes up the picture of the measure, but it is now not the separate proposition, but the whole system of propositions that is viewed as a measure. When I measure a certain point, I do so not merely by the one mark on the measure that touches it, but by the whole connected system of marks. If I know that the point lies next to mark 10, I know also that it does not reach so far as 11, 12 etc. The system by which the coloured speck is logically measured, writes Wittgenstein, is such that fx can only be true for one value of x (e.g. either $f(g)$ or $f(r)$). In the writing of his *Tractatus*, he continues, he was not as yet aware of this. 'I . . . believed then that all inferences rested on the form of the tautology. I had not then seen that an inference can also have this form: someone is 2 metres tall, therefore he is not 3 metres tall. This was connected with my belief that elementary propositions were mutually independent; from the existence of one state of affairs it was not possible to infer the non-existence of another state of affairs' (*Ph.B.*, p. 317).

It was shown earlier how in the *Tractatus* Wittgenstein presents an atomic view of language, as constructed like a mosaic, but also how, at a deeper level, he gives a more connected, organic picture of language. The possibilities according to which certain elements in propositions may take place, or according to which the objects in a state of affairs may occur— which is to say nothing about whether in fact they do occur in a given case—form one logical network. Wittgenstein now takes this a step further. He explores the elements of propositions more fully, and considers logical notations with richer content, that is to say, which show something of the friction with the concrete facticities of the world (e.g., '$f(g)$' for the greenness of a speck, and potentially, with another kind of measure, for the pitch of a note, etc.). But now the matter has become so much more complicated that it is evident there can and must be more than *one* use of logical measures. Atomism begins to vanish, and language, even at the elementary level, begins to acquire the features of an organism. But for this reason language becomes chameleon-like—the same signs and words can display very different application possibilities (it can be said, e.g., that two sounds are heard at the same place and at the same time, so that: $f(g)$ & $f(b)$).

This attempt to probe into the depth grammar, concealed under the surface of an over-controlled language, which leads only to mental cramp, is carried out in the analysis of language-games. This model or paradigm for explaining the multiformity of language is first discussed in detail in *The Brown Book* (dictated by Wittgenstein in 1934–35). He begins here with a very simple language, constructed, it would appear, in a particularly atomistic fashion, but implying in the way it is used a critique of his own logical atomism. It is a language with few words, like 'brick', 'slab', etc. These words refer to objects like bricks, slabs, etc. This certainly looks like logical atomism, with its doctrine that the elements of language reflect data in reality. But then the language-game begins. A builder calls 'Slab' to his assistant, who then brings him the object in question. A certain amount of training is needed in order to understand that on hearing a certain word one is supposed to perform some action or other, just as a child learns the use of words through some form of demonstrative teaching. The language-game can be extended, so that communication is established between the builder and his assistant with such phrases as 'Five bricks', 'That slab', 'First slab, then brick', etc. (*B.B.B.*, pp. 77–83).

Now how is this simple model a critique of logical atomism? There is no question here of a static reflection of things in words. Rather, there is a total, dynamic pattern of words and actions. 'Brick' is not a description, but an order or an appeal. It does not belong to descriptive language, which says what is and what is not the case, as was supposed in the *Tractatus*, but to language which does something, and generally to a context of social activity. It is precisely in this way that the language-games that Wittgenstein introduces in his later works form a critique of the logical period. Words are not separate entities here, mere names of isolated objects, but part of a lattice of human actions, where language itself can be a form of action. The function of language, therefore, is wider than that of giving descriptions which are true or false. In particular cases, language does name or describe, but one should also take account of the many other uses of language, such as Wittgenstein mentions in his *Philosophical Investigations*: giving orders, framing conjectures, making up a story, play-acting, telling a joke, translating, praying, cursing, greeting. It would appear, on the surface, that the 'same' forms of words recur, such as verbs and nouns, yet in terms of its depth grammar each word has a different function. 'Here the term "language-*game*" is meant to bring into prominence the fact that the *speaking* of language is part of an activity, or of a form of life. . . . It is interesting to compare the multiplicity of the tools in language and of the ways they are used, the multiplicity of kinds of word and sentence, with what logicians have said about the structure of language. (Including the author of the *Tractatus Logico-Philosophicus*.)' (*Ph.I.*, §23.)

Since language is seen less as a mosaic and more as a living organism, and since it no longer needs to be judged from a single view-point, that of a pellucid logic, but from the many view-points of everyday life, it proves impossible to draw a sharp line between one use of language and another. It is difficult to decide exactly what can and what cannot be called a 'game', says Wittgenstein. The same is true of a particular use of language. One discovers in the various language-games what Wittgenstein calls a 'family resemblance'—and one can never tell exactly just where the resemblance lies. This entails a new method, which is in some respects like the phenomenological method and which analyses a number of concrete examples. It investigates the many 'logics' of everyday language, starting with certain puzzles and gathering others around them which have certain family features in common. Moreover, Wittgenstein lays great emphasis on the practical aspect of such an analysis. Just as a medical student (to use Ryle's example) cannot learn medicine simply from a handbook, but must have attended a number of operations and must then have performed some himself, so Wittgenstein does not propose to teach a theory, but a certain skill. In that respect he continues the philosophical work of Moore, whose chair at Cambridge he occupied in 1939.

A central theme of Wittgenstein's investigations turns on the concept of 'meaning'. Even in the *Tractatus* he moved away from the current theories of Frege, Meinong, Husserl, Russell and Moore, who conceived meaningful words as 'names' for something else (things, persons, values, etc.). The theory of naming was maintained in the *Tractatus* only with respect to the 'objects' that may occur as elements in a proposition, such as 'thing', 'speck', 'sound' (see Chapter Two). Certainly, 'Fido' can be the name of the dog Fido and 'B.R.' can be thought of as the name of the organization that looks after the British railways. But even in such language-games (giving names) it is clear that the family resemblances are sometimes remote, that 'Fido' functions differently as a name than 'B.R.'. Different again, though not as names, are such variously applicable terms as 'railway yard', 'railway accident', 'railway regulations', etc. Surface grammar would suppose, mistakenly, that these words were equivalent in meaning. But as soon as we pay attention to the use and to the rules of application, the differences become evident. To use the same word is not necessarily to give the same meaning. The meaning of a bishop in a game of chess—a favourite example of Wittgenstein's—cannot be discovered by investigating the material of which the piece is made. Instead, one must follow the moves that can be made with the bishop and the rules it is governed by. 'Bishop' is not the name of a piece of ivory, but a function within a context of rules.

The same can be said of so-called ostensive definitions

(definition by pointing to the object referred to), that were mentioned in Chapter Two. To point to something is to give a meaning to a certain expression. If I say, 'This is tove', pointing to a round wooden pencil, someone can guess that 'tove' means 'pencil' or 'round' or 'wood', etc. But if I then use this word while pointing to a red woollen thread, and if the other person remembers that the pencil also was red, he can interpret 'tove' to mean 'red'. This is to say that an ostensive definition is not able of itself to give meaning to a word as an unambiguous naming of an object. On the contrary, it must be preceded by a long process of uttering sentences, pointing things out, and even perhaps taking someone by the hand and 'showing' him, if the meaning of a symbol is to be made clear to him. Wittgenstein gives many examples of this in his *Blue and Brown Books*. He shows how, for example, a child comes to learn a language—he might also have referred to modern techniques in teaching a foreign language by way of audio-visual aids. There is a direct relation between learning the meaning of a word and learning how to apply that word correctly.

'What is the meaning of a word?' This is one of those questions that produces mental cramp, says Wittgenstein, because immediately we look in the wrong direction, trying to find some substance or other to correspond to the noun ('meaning'). We then imagine that language consists of two parts : an inorganic part—the signs employed—and an organic part—the understanding of these signs, which is supposed to take place 'behind' our perception of them in an occult independent medium, the mind. To arrive at a meaning, says Wittgenstein (in a polemic against Frege's conception of self-subsistent meanings), one would have to add to the dead signs something immaterial, an ethereal meaning. As if the 'meaning' were to be thought of as something alongside the sound or the mark on the paper! No, the meaning, which gives the sign life, does not exist apart from the sign, but is precisely the use that is made of the sign. The use may vary, and it is subject to the rules that may happen to arise in the various activities of life—the language-games. (*B.B.B.*, pp. 1–25.)

Seen from another point of view, this position might be called instrumentalism. This is clear already in the *Philosophische Bemerkungen*. Words are like levers, that can be used for different purposes: one may be used as a crank, another as a switch, and a third as a pump handle. Apart from their use they are not levers at all, but only rods of a similar type. It is only in their use that they have meaning as levers, just as words also acquire meaning within the whole context of their use (*Ph.B.*, pp. 57–62). Words are much like tools in a tool-box. When viewed in this way, they can look deceptively alike. It may not be so obvious how each of them is to be used, particularly, Wittgenstein would add, if we begin to philosophize. It is only when we take the tools in our hand or watch closely how the mechanic handles them that their meaning becomes clear. This meaning will prove to be far more variegated, with many more surprises, than we expected (*Ph.I.*, §11–15). The measure becomes one of many tools, and an illustration of an *extra*ordinary language, like the language of mathematics—we shall go into this further in the chapter following. Yet we have before us a whole boxful of tools, with a great diversity of possible uses, relevant to the practice of life.

Within this wider field of investigation Wittgenstein develops themes that were already present in the *Notebooks* and the *Tractatus*. There, the meaning of a proposition lay in the possibility of its being true or false. Now language is far more than merely descriptive, and statements of fact, which can be true or false, form only a small and special part of the complex of linguistic activity. In the *Tractatus* there were composite propositions that were always true, viz., logical laws or tautologies, which Wittgenstein considered important, but also degenerate, as compared with normal, contingent propositions (e.g. 'it is raining'), which provide information. In his *Philosophische Bemerkungen* this field is already somewhat widened, on account of statements about the speck which cannot at the same time be both red and green. In the later books the case of invariably true judgments is extended yet further. There are a number of statements in ordinary usage that actually say nothing, give no information, because they follow directly from the rules we employ, and not from the application we can make of such rules. Wittgenstein calls these 'grammatical judgments'. To fail to understand this and to treat these judgments as pieces of information is to generate a philosophical puzzle.

A simple example of this is given by a person who says, 'I am *so* tall' and then indicates his height by placing his hand on top of his head. Another, rather illuminating example is the statement: one plays patience on one's own. But there are many less obvious cases of grammatical judgments. An example is: 'I can't feel your pain.' Misled by surface grammar, one might imagine it was the same sort of statement as, for example, 'I can't put your shoes on.' In this case one supposes that the inability to feel the pain and the sensations of another person is some kind of physical impossibility. Philosophically, this produces an untiable knot, for if one can never have the feelings and inner experiences of another, then one can never know for certain whether the other person has them. This poses the problem of solipsism, the doctrine that I can be certain only of my own existence and must always be in doubt concerning the existence of other people; they appear only as part of my mental world, but whether they also have a mental world I am in no position to decide. Wittgenstein has faced this problem in almost all of his works: in the *Tractatus* in the form of the statement that the world is my world, but he argues that the 'I' or subject is not something to be encountered in the world or to be expressed in language (see Chapter Three).

In *The Blue and Brown Books* and in the *Philosophical Investigations* the point is discussed in the broader terms of linguistic analysis. A statement like 'I can't feel your pain' is not to be compared with physical statements about a shoe not fitting or a weight being too heavy. It is not asserting anything that could be found in the world, but what is entailed by the rules-for-use that govern the meaning of terms like 'pain', 'experiences', 'sense-data'. The structure of such statements is not on a level with physical statements of fact, such as 'You won't get two yards from this piece of material', but on a level with tautological statements, such as 'You won't get two yards out of fifty inches.' For the last statement does not establish something that can be factually true or false, but says simply what is already implied in the system of measurement as such. The case is analogous with words like 'pain'; their grammar or rules-for-use are such that they are always meant in the sense of my own pain, and that if someone says 'I can't feel your pain' he is saying the same sort of thing as when he says 'I can't play patience with you.' The statements do not refer to physical impossibilities and do not imply a solipsistic philosophy. They only make explicit what is already implicit in the rules of the game.

By this kind of analysis Wittgenstein tries to settle the problems of metaphysics, at least as these have been discussed in traditional philosophy—as statements of some kind of superphysics. 'When philosophers use a word—"knowledge", "being", "object", "I", "proposition", "name"—and try to grasp the *essence* of the thing, one must always ask oneself: is the word ever actually used in this way in the language-game which is its original home?—What *we* do is to bring words back from their metaphysical to their everyday use' (*Ph.I.*, §116).

Everyday use is very flexible, however. Unlike logical operation rules and divisions of measures, the grammatical limits of words in ordinary language may be continually modified. Would it not be possible to play a form of patience in which two players took part? It is only a question of how much one can alter the rules without losing the meaning. Suppose that someone talks of having an 'unconscious toothache'. We ask what such a stretching of the word 'toothache' could mean. But the scientist will say, according to Wittgenstein: 'Surely it's quite simple; there are other things which you don't know of, and there can also be toothache which you don't know of. It is just a new discovery.' We shall not be satisfied with this answer, but neither shall we know what to say against it. We must analyse the meanings, and thus the ordinary use, of terms like 'pain', 'to know', 'unconscious', and see how far the analogy between these uses goes. It might be necessary to construct a new notation, in this case to use other terms than 'unconscious toothache', in order to take account of the new discovery without stretching the 'grammar' of the existing terms intolerably (*B.B.B.*, p. 23).

Wittgenstein compares the grammar of ordinary language with a pair of scales. We can weigh something on a pair of scales, and we can express something in language, for example, feelings of pain. But it is only the pair of scales or the grammar that enables us to do this. The scales and the grammatical rules are public, results of an agreement in society. What is weighed in them can be private. The meaning of private experiences, expressed in language as 'pain', 'inner experience', etc., is learned gradually. A child, for example, might learn this—in a social context where such feelings are expressed—by pulling a face or shouting 'Ow!'. This is to say that a strictly private language is impossible, for every meaning has a social background, and is acquired by practising the language-game. Consider Wittgenstein's illustration of the chess game. Two people are playing. A child runs into the room and playfully moves one of the pieces so that checkmate is reached, which neither of the players had then thought possible. Must we now say that the child, who had never played chess, had made a masterly move? No, for meaning is not a substance, an isolated datum, but issues from a knowledge of the rules. Another example: at a chess party one of the players has put a paper crown on the head of the queen. The other player asks why he has done this. He replies that for him this little crown gives a very special meaning to the queen. The other asks if he therefore intends to make some other moves with his queen than those established by the rules of chess. He replies that this is by no means his intention and that he will follow precisely the same rules as he would do without the crown. The other person then replies, with some justice, 'Then this crown does not have what I call "meaning".'

Why Wittgenstein now rejects his earlier view of meaning as naming objects was explained at the beginning of this chapter. When the builder says to his assistant, 'Brick', even when no bricks are available, the meaning is quite clear without there being a bearer of the meaning, because the meaning issues from the rules that govern this language. One might say that the substantial conception of meaning is abandoned for a functional conception. It is now evident that Wittgenstein is no less concerned to deny that meaning is derived from inner experience, and for the same reasons. The rules with which the meaning of words are connected are public. It is therefore quite possible that the meaning might still be recognized when there is no accompanying inner experience at all. If we have to buy some material of a very special colour, it might be useful to take along a sample of the colour, but if we simply want to buy a pound of red apples, a sample would be quite unnecessary. Similarly, we might sometimes have a mental picture of a colour, but normally, in selecting the red apples from the green, for example, we should not first mutter the word 'red' to ourselves and then consult the red image in our mind. No, we just pick the red apples from the green. The 'grammar' of this is again different from that of physical objects. The distinction might be clearer from two examples of Wittgenstein's. Someone is looking for a chain, which he finds eventually in a box. He could well say, 'If only I'd looked in there before, for the chain was lying there all the time.' At a fireworks display a rocket is fired which gives an extremely loud bang. 'The bang was much louder than I'd expected,' someone says. But there is no question in this case of his having an inner experience of a bang, 'lying there all the time', and which he might compare with the actual bang. This 'grammar' of physical objects does not apply here, and the question, 'Did you have a mental image of a bang to compare with the bang of the firework—you did say that it was louder than you'd expected?' is meaningless.

Elsewhere (*Ph.I.*, §293), Wittgenstein compares this whole problem of mental images, that are supposed to give meaning to words, with the following game. A number of people have a box with a beetle inside. Each person can look in his own box, but in no one else's. They tell each other what their beetles look like, what colour they are, and so on. This language-game can continue smoothly, even if all the boxes are empty. The thing in the box, which must not be public, accessible to others, is not essential for the game. The meaning of the words depends, not on their referring to certain objects, but on the rules of the game. ' "But you will surely admit that there is a difference between pain-behaviour accompanied by pain and pain-behaviour without any pain?"—Admit it? What greater difference could there be?—"And yet you again and again reach the conclusion that the sensation itself is a *nothing*."—Not at all. It is not a *something*, but not a *nothing* either! The conclusion was only that a nothing would serve just as well as a something about which nothing could be said. We have only rejected the grammar which tries to force itself on us here. The paradox disappears only if we make a radical break with the idea that language always functions in one way, always serves the same purpose: to convey thoughts—which may be about houses, pains, good and evil, or anything else you please.' (*Ph.I.*, §304.)

The point is then not to force one (physical object) use of language to suit all cases. So Wittgenstein also rejects a use of language that assumes that there is *only* physical behaviour, unaccompanied by inner feelings. He is not, he assures us emphatically, a behaviourist, and for the reason that one cannot say that there are no inner feelings behind the external behaviour, in the way one says, on opening the box, that there is no beetle inside after all.

To summarize: Wittgenstein does not derive the meaning of such terms as 'red', 'pain', 'hope' from internal conditions of mind, to which these words would refer, as names refer to objects (e.g. 'Fido', 'B.R.'). The meanings of words do not stem from private *a priori* experiences (like the imagined bang that is later compared with the real one), but from the entire social convention, which is public, and which provides the scales where inner experiences can be weighed, that is, expression in language. However, this is not at all to do away with the distinction between uttering words with and without attendant mental images, or manifesting a behaviour patter, that of toothache for example, which is and is not accompanied by genuine feelings of pain. Only, this cannot be expressed according to the same rules that govern talk of beetles in boxes.

The way has now been opened to a new field of investigation. What forms of language enable one to make the distinctions just mentioned? Perhaps they cannot be expressed in language, but can only be shown, like the metaphysical problems that Wittgenstein spoke of in the *Tractatus*? It should be said at once that in his later work language is far more flexible, subtle and multiform, from which it follows that the difference between what can and what cannot be said can no longer be so sharply defined—though it is not entirely absent, as we shall see in the next chapter. At any rate, Wittgenstein does suggest ways in which we might analyse forms of language which are not merely descriptive. And here contemporary analytical philosophy has found its programme.

Two themes in the investigation deserve to be mentioned in this context, if only briefly. The first is that of intention. (The importance of this has been noted by various writers, in particular by Miss Anscombe.) The older, narrower conception of language and verification suffered shipwreck on this, among other difficulties. For it is clear that there is a difference between doing something with and without intention, and that intention, as a concern for something in the future, is an extremely real factor in human action and language. But to say that it is real is not to say it is a phenomenon which accompanies the spoken words or the visible and verifiable actions. Wittgenstein was already occupied with this problem in 1929, and he then saw an affinity between the concept of an order that has yet to be carried out and the concept of intending an action before it is done. The case of expecting something to happen is linked with this (*Ph.B.*, pp. 58–60, §§13–16). The separation of will (which cannot be said, only shown) from idea (which can be said, given logical form) is still relevant here, though the will would nevertheless affect the use of language. This is clearer still in his later work. Words like 'intending', 'wanting to say something', have their own kind of grammar; they are governed by rules that do not imply that 'behind' what is said or done we must postulate something else, viz., intention. When someone talks about his intentions he does of course tell us something about himself, and something more than can be represented by a description of physical, verifiable action or behaviour—think of the person who assures us: 'But I really meant what I said.' (Cf. *Ph.I.*, §§588–92, 656–60.)

This touches on the second problem area, about which Wittgenstein has written a great deal, namely, the meaning of the word 'I'. Here again, there is a peculiar use of language. According to the *Tractatus*, the 'I' was not an object to be encountered in the world, whereas now it assumes its own function within the world of language, and so it can be 'said'. True, it is not a name for an object. 'I' is a different kind of reference to 'L.W.', says Ludwig Wittgenstein. It is not a person's name; even less does it refer to a kind of substance hiding inside a person, and to which he could point by saying 'I'. So there is a clear distinction between the following sentences, though according to their surface grammar they look very much alike: 'He has serious toothache' (a piece of information about a certain person; to ask in reply 'Are you sure of that?' makes sense), and 'I have serious toothache' (not a piece of information about a certain person, and to ask, 'Are you sure of that?' is nonsensical). (Cf. *B.B.B.*, pp. 66–7; *Ph.I.*, §§404–10.) The word 'I', therefore, cannot be used in language in just the same way as a name; a statement like 'I don't know if I or Mr. N.N. is in pain' is impossible. However, 'I' does have a function of its own in language, because, among other things, it makes it possible to draw attention to oneself ('Who's calling there?' 'I am') or to give names to persons ('I am L.W.', 'I am N.N.', etc.). So 'what is shown' finds its way into language. What is more, these less manageable and often misleading tools of language, so easily generating philosophical puzzles, are necessary for the handling of simpler, more descriptive sorts of language. Here Wittgenstein is again looking for paths through the labyrinth of language.

CHAPTER FIVE

Forms of Life

' "But then what does the peculiar inexorability of mathematics consist in?"—Would not the inexorability with which two follows one and three two be a good example? —But presumaby this means: follows in the *series of cardinal numbers*, for in a different series something different follows. And isn't *this* series just *defined* by this sequence?—"Is that supposed to mean that it is equally correct whichever way a person counts, and that anyone can count as he pleases?"—We should presumably not call it "counting" if everyone said the numbers one after the other *anyhow*, but of course it is not simply a question of a name. For what we call "counting" is an important part of our life's activities. Counting and calculating are not—e.g.—simply a pastime. Counting (and that means: counting like *this*) is a technique that is employed daily in the most various operations of our lives. And that is why we learn to count as we do: with endless practice, with merciless exactitude; that is why it is inexorably insisted that we shall all say "two" after "one", "three" after "two" and so on.—"But is this counting only a *use*, then; isn't there also some truth corresponding to this sequence?" —The *truth* is that counting has proved to pay.—"Then do you want to say that 'being true' means: being usable (or useful)?"—No, not that; but that it can't be said of the series of natural numbers—any more than of our language— that it is true, but: that it is usable, and, above all, *it is used*.'

Remarks on the Foundations of Mathematics,
pp. 3, 4, §4

FORMS OF LIFE

In the last phase of his activity, crystallized in the *Philosophical Investigations* and the book cited above (abbreviated: *F.M.*), Wittgenstein looked again at the relation between thought and reality, but now as a relation between language and forms of life. And also, as at other times in his life, he turned his attention to the language of mathematics. A number of things contributed to this renewal of interest. One was the intuitionism in Brouwer's mathematics, where the provability of a theorem was connected with logical intuition and constructibility. Another was the investigation of Gödel, which showed that theorems of a certain kind—within mathematical problems related to the question of infinity—were unprovable in principle. The discussions that Wittgenstein had at the end of the 'twenties with his friend, the mathematician, F. P. Ramsey, had an important influence on him. His new and growing insights came to a break-through, when in March 1928 in Vienna he attended two lectures by the Dutch mathematician—one of the founders of intuitionism in mathematics. One of the lectures was entitled 'Science, Mathematics, Language'. Here Brouwer developed his ideas on mathematical language: this is man's attempt to subject the world to his will, as a snake paralyses his prey with a look. Language is primarily action, and must be thought of in terms both of the will and of society. As a result, language is never exact and even mathematics cannot achieve complete exactness. Logic is more a by-product of mathematics and not all logical rules (in particular, that of the excluded middle, *tertium non datur*) need obtain in mathematics, with its problems of infinity. Many of these ideas are to be found in Wittgenstein's later work, although he does deny the necessity of intuition.

Wittgenstein's view can be summarized briefly as follows. He is clear, to begin with, that language is applied differently in mathematics than in most cases of everyday language—this will later be explained by reference to the question whether mathematical rules are 'ready-made', waiting to be discovered. He tries to show, further, how mathematical statements may be viewed as measures, which have a logical meaning in themselves, but only acquire practical value in so far as they are applicable in life. Accordingly, he does not see mathematics as the discovery of existing truths, but as an instrument, which must be handled inexorably. It carries with it a strong 'must', but then only because people are persuaded to follow a rule. The 'must' is therefore not physically determined, but depends rather on a language-form or language-game, in which persuasion plays a part. He is now further removed from the standpoint of the *Principia Mathematica* of Russell and Whitehead, because he insists repeatedly (e.g., in *Philosophische Bemerkungen*) that the equations of mathematics are not to be assimilated to the tautologies of logic (cf. *Tractatus*, 6·22), and thinks it is possible, if not useful, to construct chains of reasoning within symbolic logic that run parallel to those of mathematics. Finally, it will be evident that such considerations take us far beyond the technical sphere of an investigation into the foundations of mathematics—which, just because of its technical character, could only be touched on here—and that, as in the *Philosophical Investigations*, they lead to far-reaching conclusions concerning the relevance of forms of life to language, science and philosophy.

What is it that makes mathematical statements so certain? In what way are they inexorable? Do they, for example, describe aspects of reality? If not, are they then purely conventional, dependent on an arbitrary consensus? Wittgenstein discussed these problems in *Philosophische Bemerkungen* and developed them more fully in his later work.

'*How do I know* that in working out the series + 2 I must write "20004, 20006" and not "20004, 20008"?' asks Wittgenstein. I know this without needing to know it in advance, that is to say, without ever before having gone over the numbers following '20004' in my mind. The problem is already present in the series: 2, 4, 6, 8, etc., and also, for that matter, in a series like + 0 : 2, 2, 2, 2, etc. For how do I know that after the five hundredth '2' the figure '2' is still the same? Part of the answer to this must be that it is all decided by the rules that one follows. This is not to say, however, that whatever may be shown from working out the rules is given in advance, 'ready-made', as it were. But I must surely, in one way or another, know it in advance, *a priori*? What Wittgenstein wishes to make clear in his *Remarks on the Foundations of Mathematics* is that doing mathematics is a matter of using a particular kind of language. It is not concerned with ready-made objects or truths, but with 'being able to go on' according to the rules.

Wittgenstein had already entered into such problems in his *Blue and Brown Books*. This is apparent from an example mentioned in the previous chapter: if, after a long search, someone finds the chain lying in the box, he can say that the chain was there all the time, thus before he discovered it. But if someone says 'That bang was louder than I thought,' he cannot then speak of another bang, which was in his imagination beforehand and with which he could compare the real bang, even though his language appeared on the surface to say this. The possibility of continuing a series is not a hidden cause of that continuation, as an inflamed mucous membrane is the hidden cause of sneezing. True, if a parrot says '2, 4, 6, 8', one doesn't suppose he could continue the series. What Wittgenstein wishes to show with these examples is that it is not a question merely of observable behaviour, of actually repeating a few numbers, but that neither is it a question of something hidden behind these operations that must be thought of as completing them. The possibility of continuation, Wittgenstein concludes, lies in the nature of the rules that govern the game. He compares this with different games that can be played with the same material, for example, a number of cards, where one game allows the use of a limited number of cards and the other an unlimited number. The difference between them lies not in the material used for the game, but in the rules which the players choose to follow.

In this connection Wittgenstein speaks of rules 'foreshadowing' all further steps that can possibly be made. It is not necessary to cross our bridges before we come to them—or to run over a whole series before we can count. He speaks also of the action of a picture at a distance, where the picture is thought of as a rule that is to be followed and applied in the future, for example, that one can always divide a certain group into two groups, in the sense of: $\lceil \Pi \ \Pi$. The problems of infinite series, of the possibility of indicating results in advance, *a priori*, of the necessity that emerges in certain sequences—all these are connected, by means of 'foreshadowing', with the nature of the rules, the applications that are made of them and the indication of the consequence of the picture or statement, which in turn is conceived as a rule. (Cf. *B.B.B.*, pp. 91–5, 141–4; *F.M.*, pp. 20, 21, §§62–7.)

A mathematical proof is described by Wittgenstein as a decision someone takes to follow a certain rule. It is not the case that a mathematical proof shows what is already established somewhere in nature, or super-nature. Even less should one interpret it psychologically, that is, as indicating the way our minds happen in fact to work. In this sense the proof is neither purely *a priori*, fixed beforehand in a realm of eternal ideas, nor purely *a posteriori*, to be read off the facts of human experience, in particular, the process of human thinking. Wittgenstein illustrates this with some simple examples: if you take up the criminal code of a certain country, you cannot tell from the code how the inhabitants of that country actually deal with a thief, for it is not a book of social anthropology. You *could* say—and this applies equally to the rules of mathematics— that *if* people follow the rules, laid down in the code or in a certain proof, they will necessarily come to that particular result. So you can say this *a priori*, though the prediction is nothing more than a further explanation of what is meant by the 'rules' and these proceed from the decision people have made to follow the rules.

Many discussions of the foundations of mathematics fail to appreciate that people do make a decision to follow the rules, and that therefore they are also free not to do so. It is supposed that certain strange consequences can emerge in mathematical reasoning because it is evident from the rule that it *cannot* be otherwise. But the 'cannot' is clearly misunderstood, in so far as it is taken to be a factual impossibility, whereas it should be taken as what is forbidden by the rules of the game. There is a similar misunderstanding with regard to logic. It is believed to be about the logical structure of the world and it then becomes a kind of 'ultra-physics', instead of a technique for converting certain statements into other statements according to a set of rules (cf. the example in Chapter Two of the conversion of '$\sim (p \text{ v } q)$' into '$\sim p$ & $\sim q$'). Even logic, Wittgenstein now says, is connected with agreements on rules and on the application and use of these rules.

The point about application, however, leads to more far-reaching considerations. For one can ask whether the rules of mathematics and of reasoning in general are therefore completely arbitrary. Does the meaning result entirely from the use, as some have taken Wittgenstein to be saying? Ryle has pointed out, with reference to Wittgenstein, that it would be wrong to suppose that meaning can be reduced to the actual usage of rules. There is more to it than this. What is important here is the way in which rules can 'do something', and can conform to the course of nature and to human society especially.

Here again, Wittgenstein takes the image of a measure to clarify the point. Within the rules of logic and of other systems everything is necessary and *a priori*; for example, that one inch can be converted into 2·54 cm. Taking up some statements from the *Tractatus*, Wittgenstein writes that such a logical conversion tells us no more than a tautology (e.g. 'p v $\sim p$'; reflected in ordinary language, 'it is raining or it is not raining'). It is the *application* of a logical measure to ordinary language, with its varied and varying meanings. The transformation of mathematics into logical rules, as in the *Principia Mathematica*, says nothing, therefore, about whether or not they are true. A trumpet—to mention another comparison of Wittgenstein's— is unusuble without a mouthpiece, which brings it into contact with the human body. Earlier, Wittgenstein had said that language was as complex as a living organism. So the question now is, how and in what circumstances—appropriate or inappropriate—is a measure or instrument employed? One can have a 'proof' filed away in the archives of language, but the question is how such an instrument is to be used. The universality of a logical proposition poses an interesting problem, but the problem is not that there must be a concrete fact that answers to this universal—there are none, for nothing is described—but rather that there is a recurrent situation in which such a logical transformation or measure can be applied.

So the investigation moves on to the field of appropriate applications. One measure is appropriate for measuring large objects, but would be inadequate for measuring the length of viruses. With a yard one can measure the length of a room, but not the distance between the earth and the sun. This is not to say that the latter is a physical impossibility. It is to say that, within such a cosmic, spatio-temporal system, this measure is inappropriate (one would have to use light signals, for example). Here Wittgenstein is anxious to avoid the all too easy equations of 'popular science', as when, for example, it presents the findings of quantum mechanics in images borrowed from the directly observable world—those of the ordinary measure or when it pictures the cosmic dimensions of relativity theory within the same, common system of measurement. That leads to paradoxes, which are only the result of applying inappropriate measures.

Take as an example the measure of arithmetic: '2 + 2 = 4'. Children learn this by adding pairs of sticks, beans, marbles, etc. and then counting the result. But now suppose that after bringing together two pairs of beans they always turned out to be five. You would say these beans were behaving rather strangely, and try to find some physical explanation. At any rate, you would consider these beans unusable for teaching arithmetic. But suppose that every object—sticks, beans, marbles, trees, cows, etc.—behaved in this way. (This example of Wittgenstein's is not quite so far-fetched as it seems—it is actually impossible to employ our ordinary arithmetical measures in the field of microphysics.) Even then, the calculation '2 + 2 = 4' is not proved false, just unusable, as Wittgenstein puts it. What he wishes to point out is that, while calculation can be explained with the help of physical objects (sticks, beans, etc.), it never depends on the behaviour of these objects: a mathematical equation like '2 + 2 = 4' and a mathematical system as such are not derived from experience, but are rather the tools by which we measure the experienced world. On the other hand, he wants to say that one must always choose appropriate measures: a measure that is difficult to apply is not for that reason false, but it needs to be exchanged for another kind of measure, for example, another system of arithmetic.

'If a ruler expanded to an extraordinary extent when slightly heated, we should say—in normal circumstances—that that made it *unusable*. But we could think of a situation in which this was just what was wanted. I am imagining that we perceive the expansion with the naked eye; and we ascribe the same numerical measure of length to bodies in rooms of different temperatures, if they measure the same by the ruler which to the eye is now longer, now shorter.

'It can be said: What is here called "measuring" and "length" and "equal length", is something different from what we call those things. The use of these words is different from ours; but it is *akin* to it; and we too use these words in a variety of ways.' (*F.M.*, pp. 4, 5, §5.)

Clearly, what has been said here is of importance not only for the understanding of the sciences and their methodology, but also for the understanding of the measures employed in our ordinary language—we too use these words in a variety of ways—and thereby in our thinking. The implications for epistemology and for philosophy generally will become clearer if we look at two aspects. The first is that a measure, a methodology, must agree with a general feature of the reality that is measured and explained. The second is that reality itself is plastic, because it, in turn, is affected by the manner in which it is measured and approached, and can therefore be remoulded by language and thought. Both aspects will be seen to come together in the theme of the forms of life to which language refers.

It must be said first of all, then, that a measure is never completely arbitrary, since it corresponds to reality; though not, in the sense of the *Tractatus*, by reflecting the 'objects' of reality with their logical possibilities. But there are obvious general facts that make measurement with a particular measure easy and useful—on the sun one would need something quite different. 'There correspond to our laws of logic very general facts of daily experience' (*F.M.*, p. 36, §118)—for example, that we can keep on demonstrating those laws in a very simple way, with ink and paper, or can teach arithmetic with sticks and beans. That is equally true of our thinking and inferring. For while we can think in a variety of ways, this does not mean that we can do so in any way we choose, because there are natural limits corresponding to the role which our thinking and inferring play in our life. One way in which Wittgenstein expresses this idea—and he returns to it on different occasions—is to speak of the intimate connection between the techniques of logic, mathematics, thought in general and human 'natural history'.

In view of these considerations Wittgenstein rejects the doctrine that is known in the history of philosophy as 'nominalism': that concepts are only arbitrarily given names, that measures and methodologies rest entirely on conventions. However, he is even less a disciple of 'realism' (conceived as the counterpart of nominalism), which maintains that concepts have an objective existence of their own. No, the meaning of concepts is linked with the rules which govern their use—this was characterized in the previous chapter as a functional definition of meaning. This use is not arbitrary, but belongs always to a context, a situation.

The concepts and the methods used are able to transform the experienced world—this was the second aspect mentioned, and needs to be explained. Consider Wittgenstein's example of the jigsaw puzzle. We have placed every piece in the puzzle but one, and this will not fit into the remaining space. Someone else offers to help, pointing out that another piece had been placed wrongly, that it seemed to fit but really did not belong there, that a few other pieces should also be moved, and so showing how the puzzle does fit if the pieces are arranged differently. Now we have not only learned to do the puzzle, says Wittgenstein, but our view of space has been changed at the same time: we have discovered new possibilities of arranging space. The same is true of geometry. It can affect, change and enrich our view of space. And the same can happen, we might add, with architecture, which can lead to a new experience and perception of space. At an earlier time in his life, during his study of engineering at Manchester, Wittgenstein had been concerned with the spatial formation of propellers. Later on, he produced a decorative sculpture, and also designed a house in Vienna.

It goes further than this. The discovery of a new proof in science involves a reorganization of experience. We discover as it were a new dimension in the space we are concerned to investigate; it is as if the scales fell from our eyes, as if we showed a fly the way out of the bottle into which it had flown (this picture reappears in the *Investigations* to show the aim of philosophy in general!). A proof says, 'This is how you must do it,' and the 'must' is like the rails laid down for a train. A proof, a way of reasoning to a conclusion, transforms our vision, redirects our experience into different channels, persuades us to take a new road with wider perspectives. Wittgenstein concludes by saying, a number of times: 'The limit of the empirical—is *concept-formation*.' (Cf. *F.M.*, pp. 121–3, §§29–33; p. 171, §14.)

In an interesting discussion of Wittgenstein's later work, Ayer has pointed out the similarity with Kant's philosophy. Wittgenstein is indeed maintaining that knowledge is constructive, that it not merely reflects or arranges experience, as classical empiricism contends, but guides and channels it. Concept-formation sets limits to what we can call experience. With Wittgenstein, otherwise than with Kant, this is a dynamic process, because the conceptual forms are not unchangeable, but make themselves apparent in a continual interchange with the general facts of experience and within human natural history. Therefore, we can never lay down once for all what is to be understood by 'logical', 'inference', 'tautology' and 'thinking'.

Furthermore, the will does not appear now to be wholly inexpressible—'the mystical', beyond the bounds of language and the world, as we find it in the *Tractatus* (see Chapter Two). Language is not only for conveying thoughts, giving information or providing clarification. Language and the measures set up by the sciences also express a decision to take a certain path and so add new dimensions to experience. One point where he agrees with his earlier position is in talking of altering and enlarging the limits of the world, but this is not now confined to what is metaphysical, in the sense of what cannot be expressed, but properly belongs to the methods of mathematics, and indeed to every arrangement of experience, from jigsaw puzzles and bricklayer's talk to the language of higher mathematics and theory of man.

Wittgenstein mentions these last two concerns in one breath, when he argues against finitism in mathematics (a denial of the role of the infinite) and against behaviourism in the theory of man (a denial of the peculiar role of inner experience; see Chapter Four). Both have this in common, says Wittgenstein, that they deny the existence of something in order to clear up certain confusions. It is clear from what has been said that Wittgenstein does not deny this 'something', but it is equally clear that he does not think of it in the traditional metaphysical sense, as something that exists in itself. The rules themselves, which govern the meaning of words like 'beforehand', 'infinite series', 'inner experience', 'soul', 'I', point to the surplus value that these words have, and which they gain from the subtle role they play in life. For they are not merely describing facts

106

or behaviour—you cannot point to 'facts' with your finger, says Wittgenstein, because you need to know what is initially involved in 'establishing' a fact (*F.M.*, p. 173, §15).

This brings us to the subject of forms of life. For what lies behind the establishing of facts? How do the very general facts that make 'measuring' possible interact with the concept-formation that transforms the empirical? Why does language consist primarily of linguistic actions by which we *do* something (like the word 'brick' in the mouth of the builder), and why must a demonstration in science be seen as indicating the consequence of a decision? How do we discover the surplus value of words—the infinite in the finite, the internal in external behaviour, the question of goodness within what is expressible in the world? The answer to this is that behind man's language and thought, and so behind his philosophy, which must be understood as a practical activity, there lies the history of man's forms of life. Not that it is *hidden* behind man's action and speech—it is precisely what is expressed by them. 'Will' and 'idea', the mystical and the logical measure, are no longer kept in watertight compartments!

In his study on the foundations of mathematics Wittgenstein frequently makes the point that to conceive the 'must' of a logical demonstration ('from this that must follow') as a physical compulsion can create only misunderstanding. We are then misled by the 'surface grammar'. If we penetrate in depth, we shall discover that the 'must' is connected with decisions and persuasions, which are in turn related to the part which certain measures play in life. Wittgenstein takes up the theme in his *Philosophical Investigations*. There is a surface grammar, which can be grasped on sight, and there is a depth grammar, which often differs from it widely and is difficult to unearth. When spoken language suggests, for example, that words are accompanied by mental pictures, in the way they might be accompanied by gestures (in a statement like: 'I meant him or her'), then it is misleading. The depth grammar shows that there is another use of language in operation, and that what is being referred to is not so much a mental picture as a whole *story*, the image itself (of a person or thing) being a function within the story. 'But the picture is only like an illustration to a story. From it alone it would mostly be impossible to conclude anything at all; only when one knows the story does one know the significance of the picture' (*Ph.I.*, §663). This depth analysis is concerned to discover what is actually given. 'What has to be accepted, the given, is—so one could say—*forms of life*' (*Ph.I.*, p. 226).

This term is evidently meant to refer to the stories that are behind the words, and which illuminate the rules by which the words acquire their meaning. Wittgenstein is not interested, so he tell us in one of his final remarks, in tracing the very general facts behind language, to which language corresponds. That would be doing natural science. But these facts are incorporated in a story, in human history. It therefore also requires more than an investigation of natural history, he adds. The forms of life are rather the manner of action shared by people of a particular time and culture.

Does this mean that Wittgenstein is advocating pragmatism, that makes the truth and meaning of language dependent on what is useful and on the quite arbitrary consensus of opinions in a particular period? It is not clear from whom Wittgenstein borrowed the term 'forms of life'—perhaps from German philosophical usage. It is certainly not impossible that he knew the study of W. Spranger, *Lebensformen* (1914), in which Spranger analysed various personality structures with reference to the various forms of value experience. Nor that he was conversant with the work of the symbolic logician in Münster, H. Scholz, who in one of his studies in philosophy of religion,

Religionsphilosophie (1921), described the 'forms of life' as differentiations of the religious consciousness. In this use of the term a 'form of life' has not so much to do with the description of factual correspondence and behaviour patterns, as with the interpretation of typical (and further reducible) attitudes. There is still something of a recognition of values, above the level of purely pragmatic analysis and behaviouristic description.

Wittgenstein himself emphatically rejects the idea that it is a question merely of what people agree on. He distinguishes here between agreement of opinions and agreement in form of life. It becomes clear (from other examples) that he is really concerned with fundamental attitudes, which can be shown on the surface grammar of language only obliquely, and then with some difficulty. This applies in particular to our attitude towards other people. It is foolish to say that the body has a soul, as if something invisible were lodged inside it, or that the body feels pain—for if someone has a pain in his hand, we do not comfort the hand, but him and look into his eyes, says Wittgenstein. That means that talk about 'a pain in the hand' and 'the body that has a soul' must not, in accordance with the surface grammar, be taken as description or judgment or opinion. There is another kind of use here. It is the depth grammar of persuasion, sympathy, and in general, of the attitude one adopts to another person—that is the deeper sense of the forms of life, the stories of human life. 'My attitude towards him is an attitude towards a soul. I am not of the *opinion* that he has a soul' (*Ph.I.*, p. 178).

This touches on a further question, to which Wittgenstein had alluded in the *Tractatus*, survival after death. 'Religion teaches that the soul can exist when the body has disintegrated. Now do I understand this teaching?—Of course I understand it—I can imagine plenty of things in connection with it. And haven't pictures of these things been painted? And why should such a picture be only an imperfect rendering of the spoken doctrine? Why should it not do the *same* service as the words? And it is the service which is the point' (*Ph.I.*, p. 178).

Wittgenstein is pointing in these statements to the great variety of ways in which language operates. There are not only descriptions in which language operates. There are not only descriptions of facts and logical rules. There are also expressions of incitement, sympathy, hope, expectation. Language *does something*, creates new insight and new paths for action. Even the establishing of facts and deciding on the measures to be used are tied up ultimately with a manner of life. The use of a word is the *life* of the word, its meaning, said Wittgenstein; similarly, it is by way of the role that they play in human life that speaking and thinking transform the world. This is not to say that Wittgenstein has now become a 'metaphysician' or an 'existentialist' or a 'philosopher of life'. He is still concerned to search out the nonsense that appears all too frequently in language. He still rejects what he calls 'ultra-physics'. He still fights against the bewitchment of intelligence through language and tries to find *some* way through the labyrinth of language. His position in this respect remains unaltered: philosophy is merely an activity, that of clarification. One must not expect it to solve the problems, only to give a clear view of them.

Yet, on the other hand, Wittgenstein does away with the sharp distinction between meaningful, logically constructed language and the meaningless language of ethics, aesthetics and religion. What he had earlier called the mystical, the inexpressible, now permeates speech. So much so that speech becomes extremely elastic, interwoven with action and attitudes to life, and yet able to give expression to the mysterious questions of the soul, the 'I', attitudes, sympathy and hope—though not in the form of a description or theory.

The shift of Wittgenstein's thinking amounts to this. He believed initially that he could determine the sense and meaning of language—terms of Frege's, which he used in different ways—on the basis of logical notation and operation rules, together with a conception of reality as built in conformity with logical possibilities. It later became clear to him that this was only a requirement that he held before language, a requirement so absolute that little progress would be made in understanding the questions of ordinary life. He recognized further that the artificial languages, such as those of arithmetic and mathematics, could not all be reduced to one, the language of logic. They constitute different measures, different rules of conduct that one decides to follow. As such they refer to their application value, and thereby to ordinary human life. It is for this reason that Wittgenstein, and with him the philosophers of linguistic analysis, such as Wisdom, Ryle, Waismann, Austin, Hampshire and, in some respects, Ayer, analyse ordinary, spoken language. Here one discovers the forms of human life. It is true that language is much more deceptive here, a maze of old streets in the centre of the town, where often one meets a blind alley. On the other hand, it means friction with the rough ground, direct contact with the reality of life. Spoken language, though lacking the logical clarity of constructed language, does bring to light, by its very richness and precariousness, those deep, human questions of an ethical and religious nature that have stirred philosophers in the past.

Therefore Wittgenstein writes that it is a mistake to look for an *explanation* where we ought to look at what happens as a 'proto-phenomenon' (*Urphänomene; Ph.I.*, §654). The purely logical investigation undertaken by persons from the circle of logical positivism, like Carnap, has been stimulated by Wittgenstein's work, but ultimately it does not share his interest. Symbolic logic and semantics are specialisms, which have become independent, and have moved outside philosophy. Wittgenstein concerns himself as a philosopher with those areas of language that he suspects have the greatest depth, even if it is the language that most lacks logical clarity and is most often misleading. 'The problems arising through a misinterpretation of our forms of language have the character of *depth*. They are deep disquietudes; their roots are as deep in us as the forms of our language and their significance is as great as the importance of our language' (*Ph.I.*, §111). This is the theme that runs through the whole of his philosophy. Some decades before he had written: 'Words are like the film on deep water' (*Notebooks*, p. 52).

In all this Wittgenstein is playing a variation on a very old theme, that of thought and being. He does so in terms of the relation between language and reality. He can dismiss the metaphysical solutions of idealism—thought forms being—and realism—being forms thought—because it is not a question of the priority of one of two mutually opposed realms. The words of language acquire their meaning in the possibilities of their application and reality itself comes to light, in its many dimensions, in the story of the forms of human life. Originally, language and reality stood over against each other, in so far as reality was reflected and projected in language, whereas now they are seen to interact—not as two realms, as fields of theoretical description, but as praxis, as human action. Originally, language was 'my world' and what could not be thought or said was 'shown' in this logical limitation. Now philosophizing ventures into the tangle of ordinary language, with its deceptiveness, bewitchment and disquietude, and it does so in order to probe the depths. It looks at ethical and religious pictures for the essential service they do in showing the way out of the labyrinth of language. It is not the mirroring of logical language, but the action of ordinary human language, which

112

employs logic and methodology as measures, that bridges the gulf between thought and being, language and reality.

Thus Wittgenstein provides his own, modern answer to problems which had been posed long before by thinkers like Plato, Leibniz, Kant and Schopenhauer. As a being gifted with speech, man operates on the world by his verbal action—in trying to find a way through life in its depths by means of his speech, he also discovers how to respond to those primary phenomena which become apparent in his forms of life. For Wittgenstein, no less than for other philosophers, the clarification of philosophical analysis is a practical affair, which may indeed have a therapeutic effect on a whole period. He therefore compares philosophy, in his last two works, with the practice of medicine. The sickness of an age is only to be healed by a change in people's way of life and the sickness of philosophical problems can only be healed by changing the way of thought.

'The philosopher is the man who has to cure himself of many sicknesses of the understanding before he can arrive at the notions of the sound human understanding. If in the midst of life we are in death, so in sanity we are surrounded by madness' (*F.M.*, p. 157, §53).

Bibliography

WORKS BY LUDWIG WITTGENSTEIN
(*In order of writing*)

Notebooks, 1914–1916, ed. G. H. von Wright and G. E. M. Anscombe, Blackwell, Oxford, 1961.

Tractatus Logico-Philosophicus (Introduction by Bertrand Russell), Routledge & Kegan Paul, London, 1922. (This publication, like the first, has the German text alongside the English; the translation from the German by C. K. Ogden was approved by Wittgenstein. In 1961 there appeared a new edition with a better, though not authorized, translation by D. F. Pears and B. F. McGuinness.)

Philosophische Bemerkungen, ed. R. Rhees, Blackwell, Oxford, 1964. (German text only.)

The Blue and Brown Books, Blackwell, Oxford, 1958. (English text only.)

Remarks on the Foundations of Mathematics, ed. G. H. von Wright, R. Rhees and G. E. M. Anscombe, trans. G. E. M. Anscombe, Blackwell, Oxford, 1956. (Parallel texts.)

Philosophical Investigations, ed. G. E. M. Anscombe and R. Rhees, trans. G. E. M. Anscombe, Blackwell, Oxford, 1953.

Zettel, ed. G. E. M. Anscombe and G. H. von Wright, trans. G. E. M. Anscombe, Blackwell, Oxford, 1967.

Notes on Knowledge and Certainty (in preparation).

ARTICLES AND LECTURE NOTES

'Some Remarks on Logical Form', *Proc. Aristotelian Society*, Suppl. 1929, pp. 162–71.

BIBLIOGRAPHY

'Notes on Logic' (1913), *Notebooks 1914–1916*. (See above. Other lecture notes are to be found in the appendix of this book, and notes of discussions with Waismann appear at the end of the *Philosophische Bemerkungen*.)

'A Lecture on Ethics' (1929), and 'Notes on Talks with Wittgenstein', *The Philosophical Review*, vol. 74, 1965, pp. 3–16, published with an English translation by Max Black.

Wittgenstein and the Vienna Circle. Conversations recorded by Waismann, ed. B. F. McGuinness, Blackwell, Oxford, 1967.

'Wittgenstein's lectures in 1930–33', notes by G. E. Moore, *Mind*, vol. LXIII (1954), pp. 1–15, 289–316; vol. LXIV (1955), pp. 1–27. Reprinted in G. E. Moore, *Philosophical Papers*, Allen & Unwin, 1959.

Lectures and Conversations on Aesthetics, Psychology and Religious Belief, ed. C. Barrett, Blackwell, Oxford, 1966.

WORKS ON WITTGENSTEIN

(*a*) *Introductions to linguistic philosophy in general:*

J. O. Urmson, *Philosophical Analysis*, Oxford University Press, 1956.

G. J. Warnock, *English Philosophy Since 1900*, Oxford University Press, 1958.

(*b*) *Introductions to Wittgenstein's thought:*

Norman Malcolm, *Ludwig Wittgenstein; A Memoir*, with a Biographical Sketch by G. H. von Wright, Oxford University Press, 1958.

J. Hartnack, *Wittgenstein and Modern Philosophy*, trans. M. Cranston, Methuen, 1965.

(*c*) *More comprehensive works on Wittgenstein's philosophy:*

G. E. M. Anscombe, *An Introduction to Wittgenstein's Tractatus*, Hutchinson, 1959.

116

BIBLIOGRAPHY

M. Black, *A Companion to Wittgenstein's Tractatus*, Cambridge University Press, 1964.

E. Stenius, *Wittgenstein's Tractatus*, Blackwell, Oxford, 1960.

D. Favrholdt, *An Interpretation and Critique of Wittgenstein's Tractatus*, Copenhagen, 1964.

J. Griffin, *Wittgenstein's Logical Atomism*, Oxford University Press, 1964.

A. Maslow, *A Study of Wittgenstein's Tractatus*, University of California Press, 1961.

I. M. Copi and R. W. Beard, *Essays on Wittgenstein's Tractatus*, Routledge, 1966.

G. Pitcher, *The Philosophy of Wittgenstein*, Prentice Hall, 1964.

G. Pitcher (ed.), *Wittgenstein; The Philosophical Investigations*, Doubleday, New York, 1966.

D. Pole, *The Later Philosophy of Wittgenstein*, Athlone, 1958 (paper 1963).

E. K. Specht, *Die sprachphilosophischen und ontologischen Grundlagen im Spätwerk Ludwig Wittgensteins*, Heft Kantstudien, Cologne, 1963; with an English translation by D. E. Walford, Manchester University Press, 1968.

W. Stegmüller, 'Ludwig Wittgenstein', in W. Stegmüller, *Hauptströmungen der Gegenwartsphilosophie*, Stuttgart, 1965 (3rd edition), pp. 526–696.

(d) An index:

G. K. Plochmann and J. B. Lawson, *Terms in Their Propositional Contexts in Wittgenstein's Tractatus. An Index*, Southern Illinois University Press, 1962.

(e) Some important articles on Wittgenstein's philosophy:

F. P. Ramsey, 'Critical Notice of the Tractatus', *Mind*, vol. XXXII, 1923. Reprinted in: F. P. Ramsey, *The Foundations of Mathematics*, ed. R. B. Braithwaite, Routledge, 1931 (New York, 1950).

BIBLIOGRAPHY

G. C. M. Colombo, Introduction to the Italian translation of the Tractatus, Milano-Roma, 1955.

M. Black, 'Critical Notice of Wittgenstein's Notebooks', *Mind*, vol. LXXIII, 1964.

O. K. Bouwsma, 'The Blue Books', *Journal of Philosophy*, vol. LVIII, 1961.

J. N. Findlay, 'Wittgenstein's Philosophical Investigations', *Philosophy*, vol. XXX, 1955.

P. F. Strawson, 'Critical Notice of Philosophical Investigations', *Mind*, vol. LXIII, 1954.

N. Malcolm, 'Wittgenstein's Philosophical Investigations', *Philosophical Review*, vol. LXIII, 1954. Reprinted in V. C. Chapell (ed.), *The Philosophy of Mind*, Prentice Hall, 1962.

P. K. Feyerabend, 'Wittgenstein's Philosophical Investigations', *Philosophical Review*, vol. LXIV, 1955.

'L. Wittgenstein: Philosophical Investigations', *The Times Lit. Suppt.*, August 1953.

A. J. Ayer, 'L. Wittgenstein: Remarks on the Foundations of Mathematics', *The Spectator*, March 1957.

G. Kreisel, 'Wittgenstein's Remarks on the Foundations of Mathematics', *British Journal for the Philosophy of Science*, vol. LX, 1958.

M. Dummett, 'Wittgenstein's Philosophy of Mathematics', *Philosophical Review*, vol. LXVIII, 1959.

(*f*) *Some articles on Wittgenstein's life and work:*

B. Russell, 'Ludwig Wittgenstein; Memorial Notice', *Mind*, vol. LX, 1951.

G. Ryle, 'Ludwig Wittgenstein', *Analysis*, vol. XII, 1951/52.

J. Wisdom, 'Ludwig Wittgenstein 1934–1937', *Mind*, vol. LXI, 1952.

F. Waismann, 'Notes on Talks with Wittgenstein', *Philosophical Review*, vol. LXXIV, 1965.

BIBLIOGRAPHY

K. Britton, 'Recollections of L. Wittgenstein', *The Listener*, June 1955.

V. Mehta, *Fly and the Fly-Bottle; Encounters with British Intellectuals*, Weidenfeld & Nicolson, 1963.

P. Engelmann, *Letters from Ludwig Wittgenstein. With a Memoir*, trans. L. Frutmüller, ed. B. F. McGuinness, Blackwell, Oxford, 1967.

(g) *A bibliography:*

A Wittgenstein Bibliography, compiled by K. T. Fann, *International Philosophical Quarterly*, 7 (1967), pp. 311–39.

Index

INDEX